GILEAN DOUGLAS

WRITING NATURE

❦

FINDING HOME

GILEAN DOUGLAS
Three ages of life:
the child, so adult;
the youth, a tomboy;
the young reporter
in charge of life.

GILEAN DOUGLAS

WRITING NATURE

FINDING HOME

Andrea Lebowitz & Gillian Milton

VICTORIA • BRITISH COLUMBIA

Canadian Cataloguing in Publication Data

Lebowitz, Andrea, 1941–
    Gilean Douglas

    Includes bibliographical references.
    ISBN 1-55039-096-1

    1. Douglas, Gilean.   2. Authors, Canadian (English)—20th century—Biography. I. Milton, Gillian, 1947– II. Douglas, Gilean. III. Title. IV. Title: Writing nature, finding home.
PS8507.O8Z7 1999   C818'.5409   C99-911169-8
PR9199.3.D582Z7 1999

The publisher acknowledges the ongoing support of the Canada Council for the Arts and the Province of British Columbia through the British Columbia Arts Council.

Cover: Channel Rock, Cortes Island, British Columbia (Gilean Douglas collection)
Interior design by Jim Bennett

Published by
SONO NIS PRESS
P.O. Box 5550, Stn. B
Victoria, British Columbia, Canada V8R 6S4

http://www.islandnet.com/sononis/
sono.nis@islandnet.com

Printed and bound in Canada by Friesens

For Gilean Douglas

Here's tae us!
Wha's like us?
Damn few,
an' they're a' deid!

Acknowledgements

Our thanks to Wayne Wiens for his patience, practical help, and technical assistance; to Zoë and Barry Miles for their encouragement and enthusiasm for the project; and to Anita Mahoney for text preparation. We are also indebted to Simon Fraser University for financial support and to the University of British Columbia for the use of Gilean Douglas's papers. Finally, we would like to thank Diane Morriss of Sono Nis Press for her faith in this book and in the goal of bringing Gilean Douglas's work back into print.

Contents

A Note to Readers

G*ilean Douglas: Writing Nature, Finding Home* is a sampler of some of the best writings of Gilean Douglas; it is also a biographical introduction to a fascinating woman who was a poet, journalist, naturalist, farmer, and feminist. Born in 1900, she lived to be 93. During her long life she went from being the sheltered and privileged daughter of a Toronto lawyer to orphan, bohemian traveller, career woman, and writer. She loved many men and married four times, but relationships never recreated the Eden-like world of her youngest years. Rather, writing—a calling she pursued from her earliest childhood—and nature offered Douglas the solace and home she sought. For the last forty years of her life, she found her place on Cortes Island, where she wrote, gardened, and worked tirelessly for many community and political organizations. She also became a mentor to younger islanders who arrived in the seventies.

Among those newcomers was one of us. Jill Milton, a long-time resident of Cortes Island, knew Gilean Douglas for the last twenty years of her life. A difference in age of fifty years did not in any way hinder the friendship that developed between the two, and Douglas named Milton her Literary Executor (perhaps because Jill is one of the few people in the world able to read Gilean's handwriting). As Literary Executor, Jill was commanded to bring Douglas's writings back into print.

The other one of us, Andrea Lebowitz, a sometime resident of

Hornby Island, teaches at Simon Fraser University. As editor of *Living in Harmony: Nature Writing by Women in Canada* (Orca, 1996), Andrea had included a selection of Douglas's writing in the anthology and needed her birthdate—a closely guarded secret during Douglas's lifetime. Andrea's quest led to Jill and the mass of papers that constitute the Douglas literary estate.

And so this project began. We felt that the richness and diversity of Douglas's writing deserved more than a modest share in a literary anthology. The mass of papers were too tempting, too full of life, love, contradiction, accomplishment, and adventure to lie fallow. A plan evolved to detail Douglas's life and return some of her writing to the public eye at the same time. The resulting collaboration has been successful not only as a writing project but also as a friendship. Contrary to some pundits, joint writing projects can work and two heads are better than one. (We have strongly felt the third presence of Douglas as well!)

Since this book is both a selection of works and a biography of a writing life, some organizational problems occurred. Douglas's life required a chronological organization, but the publication dates of her works did not always coincide with their composition nor with the life experiences from which they were drawn. Consequently we decided to reprint the works in the chapters that record the part of her life on which the writing is based. For example, *Silence Is My Homeland*, a book about Douglas's life in the mountains, was not published until 1978 but an excerpt from it appears in the chapter on the 1940s, when the work was first drafted. (In fact, Douglas had first tried to publish *Silence* in the late 1940s but the book, which records the life of a solitary woman in nature, was not deemed "publishable" until the 1970s, by which time attitudes toward women and nature had changed. Its publication is also a testimony to Douglas's persistence as a writer.)

Another issue of placement concerned selections from Douglas's seven books of poetry. Douglas was a prolific poet who first made her reputation through this genre. Her poetry is written in the nineteenth-century tradition of Romantic Poetry and explores the great themes of nature, love, and mortality. As with many of Douglas's other writings, poems composed in her early years were not collected into books until much later. An additional complication was that the poems cannot be as closely aligned to events in her life as can her works of nature writing. We decided to place the poems where we felt they best complemented the major concerns of Douglas's life.

A further challenge was selecting from her countless journalistic works, some of which exist in many versions. She constantly reworked her articles and sent them out to many different magazines and newspapers, for this was one of her main sources of income. She was a long-time feature writer for the *Vancouver Sun* and the *Victoria Daily Colonist* (later *Times Colonist*), and over her long life she published in over two hundred periodicals. In addition, the articles were often a springboard for the broader book form. At the time of her death, she was working on three collections: a sequel to *The Protected Place*, which would further explore her life on Cortes Island; a collection of articles she had written on life along the coast of British Columbia in the 1950s; and a group of character sketches of people living in the Cascade Mountains in the 1940s. Where possible, we chose to reprint articles that Douglas herself had selected or rewritten for inclusion in these various planned collections.

A final problem concerned the interpretation of Douglas's life through her writing. It is always dangerous to assume that a writer's work, even when apparently autobiographical, is transparently true. Douglas's work is no exception; she often recast events of her life in fictionalized or distanced versions. Yet, with this in mind, it is both useful and interesting to read Douglas's writings juxtaposed with excerpts from her diaries, letters, and unfinished autobiography. In doing this it becomes clear that certain themes recur.

The desire for peace and stability, the fundamental dedication to writing, and the celebration of the natural world come together in a lifelong search for a home—a home she finally found in the silence and solitude of nature, rather than in a more usual domestic relationship. We hope this book conveys to you, the reader, the fascinating complexity of Gilean Douglas as a woman and a writer, and instills in you a longing for the natural world that so inspired her.

—ANDREA LEBOWITZ AND GILLIAN MILTON

CHAPTER 1

A February Face

*E*very childhood is a reconstruction of memory, but for a writer like Gilean Douglas, whose stock-in-trade was observation and recollection, childhood provided the first rich harvest of imagination. In her unpublished and unfinished autobiography, *A February Face*, Douglas revisited the past and acknowledged, "It is hard to tell where memory leaves off and imagination begins."[1] A writer from her earliest days, Douglas constantly composed—and recomposed—the world around her.

Creating her own narrative of origins was a fundamental first step in this grand process of living a life, but the plain facts were grand enough. Born in Toronto on February 1, 1900, Gilean was the only child of Eleanor Constance Coldham and William Murray Douglas.[2] Hers was a wealthy and socially prominent family, and throughout her life, Douglas took great pride in her family background. On her mother's side, she traced her lineage back through Charles VI of France, Henry VII of England, and Llewellyn of Wales, while her father's family descended from Sir Robert Douglas.

Her father, a lawyer later appointed Queen's Counsel, was a respected man in Toronto society; her mother, almost always called Nellie, was a notable society beauty from an elite family of Toledo, Ohio. Married in 1898, the young couple was the toast of Toronto society. *Toronto Life* proclaimed Nellie and her sister the "brides of the year," and city newspapers carried detailed accounts of the social activities of "the American Beauties."[3]

Although Douglas was born into a new century, the world was still largely one of the past in its social organization and material aspects. It was a society characterized by marked class distinctions. For some, those were the days of horses and carriages, of afternoons spent calling, of tea dances and midnight suppers that were later mentioned in the social Blue Book. The Queen still reigned, and in this Canadian outpost of empire, the manners and mores of England's Victorian era were intact. Well-to-do Canadians lived in grand houses maintained by servants, and they travelled abroad or made summer retreats to country houses and elegant resort hotels.

For others, it was a time of limited privilege indeed. Women did not have the right to vote and, although some Canadian universities had opened their doors to female students in the 1880s, many women were still poorly educated. The issue of whether women should work was widely debated—for the elite. The poor had no choice. Middle- and upper-class women who wished for or needed financial independence had few opportunities, aside from nursing and teaching. However, new opportunities for employment as clerks, typists, and telephone operators, coupled with the demands of the First World War, meant that more women would soon enter the work force.

Decades later, Douglas drew on remembered childhood events in her essays. One of these, "Once Upon a Christmas," gives a flavour of her life as a little girl.

> When I was very young, we lived on the edge of a large city which is now a metropolis, and some of the loveliest moments of my life have been spent in an outlying forest at midnight. My grandfather, who never did things in the usual way, would wake me up on Christmas Eve, and we would tiptoe out of the house to find his saddle horse, Bonny Briar, and the sleigh with the big fur robes waiting for us in the silent street.
>
> Then—whoop and hurray!—we were off through a night of stars and snow with my shouts of joy startling the air of a quiet countryside. These days, we would have a posse of police chasing after us, but in those fairytale times of at least a little empty space, it seemed as though we owned the world in all its Christmas splendour. For it was always at Christmas that Grandfather came, so he and I could leave the mundane town and find a fairy forest once again.
>
> The forest was a tract of wild land in a ravine though which a small stream ran—the accompaniment to a wild bird's singing, the woodsy sound of mice and the very occasional human. But on a December night with Christmas in the

air, it was full of mystery and delight. It was a white wonder, and I hugged it to my childish heart.

Sometimes Grandfather had snowshoes packed in the sleigh and, always, he had delicious tidbits of my favourite foods—though in fact I liked anything edible as long as it had chocolate in it. So we nibbled by the light of the moon and chased our shadows as they ran over the snow, always just out of reach as they are, those owls and moons and shadows, now that the ravine is filled with occupants and all the trees have gone but always safe and steady in my heart.

On Christmas Eve, I slept in the guest room, and although I was allowed to sleep late on Christmas morning, I never did. With daylight, I was up and running through the house and particularly up to my nursery's locked door, beyond which the big Christmas tree stood in all its bedazzlement of evergreen and tinsel.

In the morning, only my special friends shared it with me. In the afternoon, the whole world could come and sometimes I felt it did. By evening, everything was quiet, though sometimes my parents gave a party. I tumbled gratefully into bed, all the time protesting that I was wide awake and ready to go again.

The nursery was my bedroom, so all I had to do was reach out my hand to touch the magic Christmas tree. I always did touch it. Then I hugged my parents, hugged my favourite dolls and went to sleep. Sometimes I said: "Merry, merry Christmas, Gilean." Outside, the whole world seemed filled with snow and moonlight. In the ravine, the small stream's voice was iced in silver, and a white silence lay on all the land. It had been such a lovely day. It was a lovely childhood.

Compared to it, my later years were like Jacob's coat. I was never quite sure where I would find myself at Christmas, but Christmas was always good. . . .[4]

While Douglas sometimes said she had little recollection of her early childhood, what she did know was that it was clearly one of privilege. Her first years were marked by travel to England and Europe as well as vacations in Canadian and American beauty spots.

In her seventh year, however, her earliest world changed dramatically with the death of her mother. As she recorded in *A February Face*:

I was playing in the nursery that day in March when my nurse—I think her name was Phyllis—came up with a funny look on her face and said that my mother wanted me. I remember I was surprised for she had been ill for days and I hadn't been allowed to go near her. I didn't want to go now.

The trauma of being taken to see her dying mother was amplified later when she realized she never really knew what her mother died of or when her illness had begun. "They told me pneumonia," she wrote, "but I know now that it couldn't have been that. Then years later, an aunt of mine said that it was some disease of the liver. That may have been right, and I know now what it might have been brought on by, but I wasn't aware of these things when Phyllis came for me." Later she may have thought that alcohol plagued her mother as well as her father, but she did not know this as a child. What she did recall was being frightened and alone: "I cried fiercely and loudly. No one could quiet me until the doctor came and gave me something."

Her fear and loneliness continued, because her father unexpectedly had to leave the very month of her mother's death. She sent him daily telegrams to keep him in reach and was relieved by his return and the advent of summer and more pleasant times.

For the next eight years, Douglas's life revolved completely around her father, and he was the beloved provider whose concern centred on his little princess.

> My father was a brilliant lawyer, and I was his only and beloved child. Daddy had very advanced ideas on nutrition and childrearing and I benefited from them. But he couldn't always bring himself to be stern when he should have been and if I said I wanted a thing it wouldn't be long before I had it.

Ada, the housekeeper, could not replace Gilean's mother, but she gave the little girl love and affection and as much guidance as the child would take.

> Yes, those were good days, for I had security and love and background and was like a little princess in her kingdom. Parents wanted their children to play with me and felt glad when they had an invitation to our house. My clothes were of the loveliest materials, and everything I had was expensive and in good taste— and I could have anything I wanted. I was all my father had to live for.

The sense of living in a childhood Eden never left her, and later, she often expressed her recollection of this paradise in terms of the physical space of home. Peace and elegance and order at home, regardless of circumstances, were the emblems of the lost kingdom.

> But always there was the house from the time I was seven. It was a very lovely and very costly house with the decorating done by someone from New York and the furnishings coming from England or the U.S. or wherever my parents could

find just what they wanted. Outside, it was burnt brick and the front door was painted white like the trim of the casement diamond-paned windows. When you went into the hall, there was a lovely carved oak chest just inside the door and the rugs were kept in there, particularly the Douglas tartan rug with the dress tartan on one side and the riding tartan of dark blue and green on the other.

Within this protected realm, the centre for both Gilean and her father was the library, which she said was really the heart of the house.

> It glowed like a heart, for the walls were hung with dark red, almost satiny, material, and all the woodwork was stained the same color. The furniture was black oak and magnificent. . . . Then there was Daddy's chair, which always stood by the table just where the lamp was. It was an easy chair covered with the same material as the walls, and it was a lovely one to curl up in. So many evenings, Daddy and I would be there after dinner, he reading and I studying at the table across from him.

This shared space was also a symbol of their mutual love for books, learning, and writing. Her father's occupation as a lawyer accounted for some of this, but he was also interested in creative writing and was president of the Osgoode Hall Legal and Literary Society. While his poetry did not often rise above the ordinary, the sheer amount of it indicated his dedication to the muse, and he conveyed this love of poetry to his daughter.

Even before she went to school, Gilean was enchanted with the world of stories and mythology. She could read by age five and devoured classic tales like those of Rob Roy and Robert the Bruce. Her love of books and reading carried into her early school years, which were spent at a private school just down the street from her house. She liked to learn and had a lively circle of school friends. "I was always over at their houses or they were over at mine," she wrote. "We edited a weekly magazine together and put on the *Iliad*."

It is telling that Douglas remembered her school days in terms of writing and drama. Storytelling came naturally to a child reared on heroic tales, and literary efforts were a common pastime for children of that era, yet her involvement with writing was more than a childhood game. "Sometimes there would be a poem in me," she wrote, "and then I would walk up and down the room muttering to myself until it came

William Murray Douglas.

Eleanor (Nellie) Constance Coldham.

*Nellie Douglas
holding baby Gilean,
March 20, 1900.*

*Nellie and Gilean in a carriage
drawn by Bonnie Briar, the
Douglases' riding and driving horse.*

The Douglas home on
Madison Avenue, Toronto.

Gilean,
at about 3 years of age.

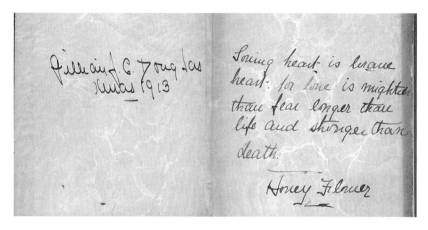

In an essay written when she was elderly, Douglas recalled turning ten: "This makes me remember my tenth birthday and the birthday book given to me by one of my three best friends. 'Love is mightier than fear, longer than life and stronger than death,' I had written on the flyleaf in a very tenish hand. I would write it again now." ("Winter, That's a Magic Word," Victoria Times Colonist, January 1992.)

out in its entirety. Then there would be such exultation in me that I would hug myself with my arms and dance a little jig."

Her sense of the imperative of writing and the pure joy in creating a poem was matched by her drive to organize and lead people and to seek an audience. These needs could all be realized in writing and performing, and she drew her playmates into her literary schemes.

> Since I was eight, we had been publishing a magazine which grew and grew with the years. I have some copies of it now which Ada saved for me. What Armoral and Katherine and Marjorie and Phyllis and the others did on it I don't know, for I seem to have written the whole thing: stories, poems, plays, jokes, the question-and-answer department and even the illustrations. . . . There were about a dozen pages—sometimes more—and the whole thing was written out by hand. It sold for five cents.

An audience of neighbourhood playmates and parents was available when the children put on the *Iliad*, and again, Gilean took centre stage as adapter, actor, and manager. But an even larger public was possible. The *Toronto News* had a children's page that published the work of youngsters and fostered their endeavours through the Canadian Beavers

Writing Club for girls and boys. Gilean joined the newspaper club and assumed the first of many *noms de plume.*

As the "Battle Maid," she made her first submission to the *News* and in later years she was proud to recall that her first piece of writing—a nature poem, since lost—was published when she was seven. In addition to taking a pen name, she disguised her handwriting and did not tell her father of her attempt at publication. One of her friends did a sketch of the Battle Maid that was published alongside her work. As the name and illustration suggest, the Maid is doughty and fearless—an identity Gilean wished for but did not always achieve.

> I used to seize the paper as soon as it came and look to see if it had been published. I can smell that newsprint now, just as I did when I pored over it at the library table. The day my letter was in, and a poem, I went flying down the walk to meet Daddy with the paper waving in my hand.

Over the course of her lifetime, Douglas used a number of pseudonyms. Some were necessary so that a woman's manuscript could be published; others she chose deliberately to portray a different voice or to sell a different type of writing. She also used her pseudonyms to comment on her own writing. As the Battle Maid, she became vice-president of the Canadian Beavers and, in that capacity, she responded to the stories submitted by Gillian (as she still was) Douglas. What is remarkable is that from her earliest years, she seemed to intuit the possibilities in changing her name. During her teens, she transformed her given name, Gillian, into Gilean, and throughout her life took new names to initiate new ways of being. From a diary entry on January 3, 1912:

> By the way, I am thinking of adding a new name to my others, though I don't know what it will be. I was thinking of Ellen, but I am not sure that I would like it. I want an uncommon one. . . .
>
> I am always making plans about A.W. and Mary and the Bs but they never come to a head and never will. I am not going to write a magazine my eyes are not strong enough but I am going on with my stories!! "The Hidden Jewels of Corba," "Do Or Die," "The Fate of the Fairy Queen"—and I have got another in my head. I may send one of my poems to the Children's Encyclopaedia and I hope they will accept it, but I don't expect so. I may send one of my stories, but they are all too long. I want to make them into a book of fairy tales and call it "Fairy Lore." When spring comes, I am going in for nature study and the different bushes and trees, and I may plant a garden. Farewell till we meet again. I am going to write.[5]

Douglas thought of herself as a writer even when she was a young girl and moved forward steadily from her first successes as a published author. Her mention of "going in for nature study" also presaged a major passion of her adult life. From childhood, she loved the outdoors. In a letter to her newspaper club, the Battle Maid wrote: "Aunt Nan, do you know I am a regular boy, that is in my tastes. I love 'roughing it,' I mean camping out, and I am always bemoaning the fact that I wasn't born a boy."[6] While she could not change her gender, writing offered a way to combine her love of nature and her desire to escape the constraints placed on girls. More basically, writing satisfied her heart in a way nothing else ever would. She assumed the writer's life as her true vocation and, as she put it in one of her last essays, all she ever wanted to do was write. Already thinking of herself as a professional in childhood, she kept the revisions of whatever she wrote, and that became a lifelong habit.

These early, triumphant literary efforts seemed to crown a perfect childhood in which the world was very much her oyster. "So there were the school days and holidays and the coming and going of the seasons," she wrote, "but the house was always there and always beautiful. . . . Ada was there to listen to my nonsense and comfort my tears, and there was always writing to turn to if my world went askew for the moment. And back of it all and all of it, really, was Daddy."

Douglas's lifelong penchant for travel started with a series of early journeys with her father, but when he travelled alone, they corresponded daily.

> Every summer we went away to the sea or the mountains or the lakes up north, and in winter Daddy always went down to Bermuda or Nassau or somewhere in the south where the warm air would help his bronchitis. He would write me every day—"My Darling Baby"—and his letters would tell me everything he was doing and seeing. They would end usually with "all the love in the world," but sometimes it would be "with as many kisses as there are stars in the sky or grains of sand on the shore." And he wrote verses about me and to me: "My Valentine, Baby's in Bathing Today." I still think they are lovely things.

Yet all was not as idyllic as it seemed. The closeness of her relationship to her father was marred by her knowledge from an early age that he had a drinking problem.

The first couple of Christmas mornings I can remember were lovely times, but later, Daddy would put down a glass to come upstairs with me. Later still, he would bring it with him and sometimes he spoke queerly and didn't seem quite steady in his walk. During those years, there were other times than Christmas when I would crouch on the big red couch in front of the library window and watch to see if he could walk straight when he got out of the taxi which had brought him home from the office. If he couldn't, I would tear up the stairs to my study and stay there and not go down to kiss him.

These withdrawals and slights were passing incidents quickly suppressed under their mutual need and love, and Douglas, for the most part, remembered her childhood as a time of warmth and security. As she entered puberty, however, a deeper sense of loneliness surfaced, perhaps caused or intensified by her first thyroid flare-up. At the age of eleven, she began to develop a goitre. The probable cause was lack of iodine in the natural environment of her birth place. Southern Ontario has low levels of naturally occurring iodine, and the practice of adding it to salt had not yet begun. However, the problem was understood and Gilean received iodine treatment. This arrested the growth of the goitre and ameliorated the symptoms which were both physical (such as sweats and racing heart) and psychological (such as anxiety). Thyroid problems were to plague her throughout her life, but for now, a loving father took care of her and all seemed well.

As she wrote on July 14, 1911, when she was eleven:

I got up at a quarter past eight, and then I wrote in my "Good Times Book," and then I got dressed and went down to breakfast. After breakfast, I read till about a quarter to one, and then I gathered up all the books on the balcony and took them upstairs to my nursery and put them in their right places. Then I packed a little, and Ada came up to get ready to go to Miss Williams, and I felt so miserable and forsaken that I began to cry. I was nervous too, I think.

Ada asked me what was the matter, but I could not tell her. It really was that nobody likes me except Daddy and Ada and my Aunt Lillie. Other people don't like me because I am not pretty and gushy, and I feel so left out of everything. But I will make them like me by living up to my standard of being clean, honourable and strong—and I vow I will never marry a man unless he measures up to my standard. Wealth and family position go for nought when measured with the three notches on my silver yardstick.[7]

Despite these brave words, Gilean could not dispel a feeling of isolation, which in some ways worsened when she moved from her

*A family
photo album
gives glimpses
into Gilean's
early childhood*

*On board
an ocean liner,
1902.*

*Gilean
and her father
in front of
a British office.*

*A donkey ride
at an English
seaside resort.*

*Dressed
for winter,
c. 1903.*

Gilean, 1904.

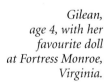

*Gilean,
age 4, with her
favourite doll
at Fortress Monroe,
Virginia.*

Gilean entertaining at a tea party, her beloved "Mammy" doll in front.

*A jolly good
golfing swing.*

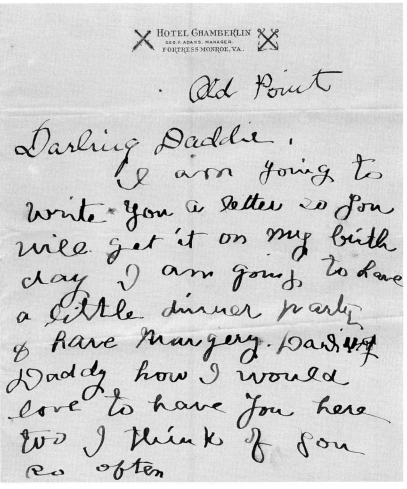

HOTEL CHAMBERLIN
GEO. F. ADAMS, MANAGER.
FORTRESS MONROE, VA.

Old Point

Darling Daddie,
    I am going to
write you a letter so you
will get it on my birth
day I am going to have
a little dinner party
& have Margery. Darling
Daddy how I would
love to have you here
too I think of you
so often

A letter from Gilean to her father, 1904.

dont peget me on my
birth day.
Your loving Darling
        Gilean X X

*Valentines
exchanged by Gilean
and her father,
preserved carefully
in scrapbooks,
show their love
for each other.*

Gilean and her father, ready for a swim.

Valentine to Gilean from her father.

My Baby is my Valentine,
No Cupid with his wings
Need hover round my heart;
My Baby worlds of pleasure brings,
Her love my love – no time can part,
My Valentine – my sweet sweetheart

Daddy

small primary school, Miss MacKellar's, to Glen Mawr. She thought that the headmistress was "an old gorgon" but soon found mentors in two teachers: Miss Stuart, who later replaced the head mistress, and Miss McPherson. These women were sympathetic to Gilean's needs and ambitions, and they remained her friends until their deaths. Yet for all this, school was not the familiar and supportive place it once had been. She felt herself to be always on the edge of the crowd, as she phrased it, and somehow isolated from life around her.

Her home world was also changing. By her early teens, her father's drinking had increased.

> The mornings when I would go into the dressing room, which always smelled of shaving soap, and watch Daddy shaving while he hummed "Bonnie Dundee" were gone, and there was the feel of it in the house and among the servants. I know how Ada worried, and I used to lie in bed hearing him come up the stairs stumbling and sometimes falling, and I would shake and put my hands over my ears. There would come that sick feeling in my stomach which still comes when there is loudness or anger or when someone I love does something which shames them. Ada became more and more the one who told me what to do, and she let me do pretty much what I wanted.

The year 1914 was a time of crisis for Gilean Douglas's private world as well as for the international world. Entering puberty with little adult guidance, she turned to the outside world for excitement, and there was plenty of change and emotion in the air as the country moved to war. When she and her father arrived at Niagara for their usual summer holiday that year, the protected world of wealthy leisure had shifted dramatically. To be fourteen in 1914 was to be thrown headlong into a whirlwind of change. Not only was Gilean facing her own personal and biological transformation, she was participating in the home-fires flurry around the war which regrettably did not end all wars, but which did end a way of life for herself and her country. From her autobiography:

> When we arrived at Niagara, it was a camp—soldiers everywhere, canteens going like mad and bandage-rolling and knitting competing with the movies. I was enchanted. Soon I was going walking with a lad of good family who was studying for the ministry and who was only nine years older than I. He thought I was eighteen. The American legion was over there for a while, and there was a major with whom I sat out and danced. I felt all turmoiled inside, but I wouldn't

let any of them even kiss me. . . . It was nice to have as many beaus as possible, but if one wouldn't stay around—well, why worry? That one was terribly hurt and bewildered never struck me.

It's funny. Children and dogs and people who are lost and bewildered can always tear my heart out, but not the men who have loved me. Partly, I suppose, the little princess wanted something else so now they didn't matter any more. . . . The other pattern of meeting people out of my own class began to work out here, for I served coffee in the canteen and my best friends that summer were some of the town girls, and they all had beaus among the officers. . . . Daddy didn't like it, but he was drinking a lot, and I know now he was not well so he never stopped me entirely. It was difficult to do anyway, with everyone being patriotic and tearing around like three fire alarms.

All that summer, she was intoxicated with life and love and was involved in a frantic round of activities that continued even after her return to school in the fall. Although her father tried to put some limits on her socializing when they returned to the city, the desire to be popular and have friends had become too strong.

I had had years of being lonely in a lonely house, of making my own fun, of living too much in imagination. And here was reality and people who wanted to dance with me and take me to movies and out driving and walking and tea-dancing, to go wherever I wanted to and do whatever I asked. I drank it all in great gulps. I was loved; I was popular. I was first with a lot of people.

This whirlwind world came to a crashing halt with the unexpected death of her father from a heart attack on January 9, 1916, a month shy of Gilean's sixteenth birthday. Suddenly, her protected world vanished, and she was on her own.

So they were all over—the years of ease and riches and assurance and the castle with its little princess and the servants to do her bidding. There would be no more coming in the white door after school or popping corn in front of the library fire or ducking for apples at Hallowe'en or trying to see Christmas gifts or studying at the mahogany desk under the green lamp with the black marble base. There wouldn't even be any more Ada.

But I didn't know all this until after my sixteenth birthday on February 1. I stayed away from school and in bed late in the mornings, and Ada pampered me and made me rest a lot. I just stayed around the house most of the time and wandered from room to room touching things, because Ada let it out that the house would probably be sold if they could find a buyer for such a big place. Then I found that I was to go to boarding school after my birthday was over. Ada tried to make the day as happy as possible for me, but it was pretty sad for both of us.

We kept listening for a step along the hall or waiting for the whiff of a cigar from the library. Everything was there except the most important thing of all.

Gilean went back to Glen Mawr as a boarder. "I hated it," she wrote. "I hated the lack of privacy most." Bereft and cut off, her emotional turmoil was matched by physical collapse. She suffered a recurrence of the same thyroid problem that had flared up earlier in her teens, but which had then been brought under control. Left untreated, the growing goitre, which was a result of a malfunctioning thyroid, added to her physical and emotional distress. Alone and uncared for, she collapsed.

> So I had a breakdown. I had a bad one. I got so I couldn't take in anything people said any more. . . . If someone had only taken me into their home then and cared for me and had had the thyroid looked after, physically and mentally! But they left me at school, and I had to get over it as best I could.

Finally, she was hospitalized, but little was done to heal her wounded heart. During the first year after her father's death, Gilean spent summers and school holidays with her aunt—her mother's sister—and uncle. Although she had always felt closer to her mother's side of the family, this arrangement quite clearly didn't work out.

> I think they [maternal aunts] both loved me, but they wanted me to go the social round, and that is where we differed. I wanted to learn cooking and a lot of useful things and to get out in the world and not be sheltered all my life and marry one of the boys of good family who always seemed a bit stupid to me. I think a lot of the trouble was that I should have been a boy. I had that spirit of adventure in me, and I had no idea then that I couldn't do anything I wanted.

She was sent to some of her father's relatives in Woodstock, Ontario, and that change was both geographical and social.

> It was another bad change to go from these relatives who had everything to the ones in Woodstock who didn't have much. They always seemed to be talking about it, too, and it was years before I realized that they were simply jealous of me because I was, or would be, very wealthy. Daddy's will, aside from a few minor bequests, had left everything to me, and it was something over one hundred thousand dollars.

But the estate wasn't settled until five years later, and as far as I knew, I was going on charity. I really wasn't, but I honestly thought that the Suydams were paying for everything and that the Douglases were doing the same. The feminine part certainly acted as though they were and as though I were a burden which could hardly be borne. Probably I was.

Her sojourn with her Woodstock relatives was not happy. She got on well with her uncle and her cousin Mac, but not with her aunt or female cousins. They were jealous of her inheritance, and for her part, Gilean didn't like being in a place where she came last instead of first. She thought of herself as a Cinderella forced to do more than her share of the household chores, and she felt unwelcome and in need of protection.

An escape, which earlier would have been possible only through marriage, was realized because it was wartime. The First World War years marked the end of the mores and manners of the old century and a change to a new international and national society. As soon as she turned eighteen, Gilean volunteered to do farm service as part of the war effort. "I had patriotism pretty badly all right, but there was probably more to it than that. I would have done a lot to get out of that house—and once I did get out, I never went back." The move to the country was liberating in many ways. She shed the claustrophobia of the Woodstock relatives, and her health improved. She spent two months at a farmerettes' camp in Jordan and then went to live and work at the nearby farm of the Rittenhouse family in Vineland, Ontario.

She enjoyed herself immensely, not least because of the number of flirtations she had and the number of hearts she won, but she also responded to the farm people and to working on the land. "I loved being with them. I worked hard, and they liked that. . . . Of course, we had some beaus too. . . . I went back and back there for visits through the years, and the welcome sign was always out for me." This was her "first experience with the country for any length of time," and it, like much else, became part of her writings. Although she had frequently vacationed in the country as a child, she chiefly remembered the small towns rather than the countryside around them. In Vineland, it was the living countryside itself that beguiled her, and she was rarely unhappy.

It is the smell of the earth I remember best at Vineland, in the early morning when the air was dewy and fresh or crisp and clear, and the scent of it in the

Photography began early.

"School days"

Gilean, age 12.

Gilean at age 13.

*In front of Glen Mawr school
(Gilean in front row, left).*

At Niagara, 1914 (Gilean fifth from left).

Gilean at age 14 (far right).

With schoolmates (Gilean in back row, second from left).

One of many beaus . . .

. . . and another.

The Rittenhouse family of Niagara, where Gilean was a farm worker in 1918.

greenhouse, that steamy perfume smell, and the tang of it in the fields. Then at night when the dew was on the grass and a little breeze was blowing, all the growing things were in it then and the water which made them grow—and even the sun. They were blended by the night into exquisite perfume.

These months in the country served as Douglas's apprenticeship in nature. Working with the land, she began her lifelong love affair with the natural world. Liberated from her background, doing work that was valuable and all the while being paid for her efforts, Gilean Douglas began to fashion a new sense of herself. It was to be many years before she could fully develop a way of life based on this self-image, but her time in Vineland served as the point at which she turned away quite naturally from her inherited style of life.

With the end of the war, Douglas returned to Toronto. Although she had decided that she wanted to be self-supporting to break free of her guardians, she was still under twenty-one and had to satisfy their wishes by boarding at Glen Mawr, her old school, while she took a stenography course. She hated the course but doggedly stayed with it. She was still there when she landed her first job as a newspaper reporter with the *Toronto News*. "I was nineteen and a newspaper woman," she wrote later, "with the world at my feet."

She found herself a reporter for Miss Dyas, "my old friend, Aunt Nan of the Canadian Beavers." Her early efforts as the Battle Maid had led her to the beginning of a career in journalism, and her endless hunger to write and be read was about to be satisfied. Her mentors, Miss Stuart and Miss McPherson, "drank a toast . . . in wine and wished me all the luck in the world."

This triumph led her to become editor of the children's page and to encourage school participation in the paper. Working hard and long, she was having the time of her life. The many hours of work each week at the paper did not stop her from conducting several flirtations, and she had different beaus for breakfast, lunch, and dinner. She was trying to have it all. "I remember thinking: I want to write, but first I want to enjoy myself. When I'm thirty and too old for that, I'll start to write in earnest."

She was also trying to have it all by becoming seriously involved with one young man while still dating others, but fate stepped in. After the paper folded on September 12, 1919, she became engaged to Grant Black. They kept the engagement secret. In her diary, she wrote: "I was jobless and, on the Sunday, I became engaged to Grant. O consternation! O joy!"[8] Undeterred by the loss of her job, she joined the Press Reporting Syndicate and began to try her hand at freelancing. Before that could come to fruition, however, she applied for the position of assistant to the advertising manager at Lever Brothers and won the job over fifty-two other applicants, some far more qualified than herself. Her salary was twenty-five dollars a week, a princessly sum—and one that led to thoughts of her own apartment.

During these years when she struggled to become independent (and indeed, for much of her life), Gilean Douglas was theoretically well off but in fact often painfully short of funds. Her father's estate of one hundred and twenty thousand dollars was significant, but since it had not been settled, she was still dependent on her guardians for the release of funds. Whether they were unwilling to increase her allowance or whether she desired to demonstrate her freedom, she found herself strapped for money and reliant on what she was earning. The Lever Brothers job offered her the possibility of getting out on her own, and she convinced her guardians to allow her to get her own apartment.

> I began looking for an apartment or a flat and went to see a lot of them. I wanted a fireplace of some sort and a balcony, and I also wanted a place that wasn't a boardinghouse. Finally, on a poor street, I found a bath flat (just use of the small bathroom) with sitting room, bedroom and kitchen. They were all very small and the furniture was old (horsehair sofa!) . . . but they were clean, and there was just the landlady and her middle-aged daughter in the house. . . . I had the use of the phone, and there was a small verandah at the back and a fireplace. Such silly things make up my mind for me! I liked looking down the hall from the top of the two steps leading to the balcony; it looked like my little kingdom to me.

> So I took it for $40. . . . Then I started painting. . . . That was when the food end suffered, for I begrudged every cent for things for the house. . . . Aunt Lillie was furious at me going to live alone and lectured Grant on it, for she thought he had influenced me. He had, in a way, but I had such a longing, too, for a place of my own. . . . I loved fixing it up, and I can see myself now standing on a chair painting the verandah ceiling with the white paint dripping down on my hair. I didn't know a thing about housekeeping, but I made things look nice with what I had.

The strong need to find a suitable place—and to create a home of her own in it—was to drive Gilean Douglas through her entire life. Eventually, it was nature that provided her with her true place and fulfilled that need, but at this earlier stage in life, she was delighted simply to feel she was a woman of the world. She was revelling in her new-found freedom. "I slept late in the apartment, had most of my meals out, saw something of the girls I had gone to school with and something of my relatives and quite a lot of this lad and that," she wrote in her autobiography.

The need to have it all and to be popular (perhaps to "find Daddy") intervened in her daily life. While she was planning her future with her fiancé, she began going out with another young man. "When I wanted something, I just closed my eyes and went after it. One day it would be like that and I would just walk over people's feelings, and the next day I would be going to all sorts of sacrifice—real sacrifice of time and money and often health—to do something for someone to make them happy. And they were both me!"

Eventually, the inevitable happened: the engagement went up in flames.

EXIT

So willfully,
So skillfully,
I played my little part;
So dolefully,
So soulfully,
You showed me all your heart.

So cooingly,
So wooingly,
We murmured of next June;
So smitingly,
So blightingly,
You found me out too soon.[9]

Then she lost the Lever Brothers job for being away from work without an excuse, and that changed her circumstances yet again.

Gilean Douglas was about to embark on a very different life from the one into which she had been born. Fiancé and father were both now gone, and there was no one to fulfill her cravings for love, attention, belonging, identity. In the summer of 1921, she returned to familiar circumstances in the Niagara area to gather herself up again before the next step.

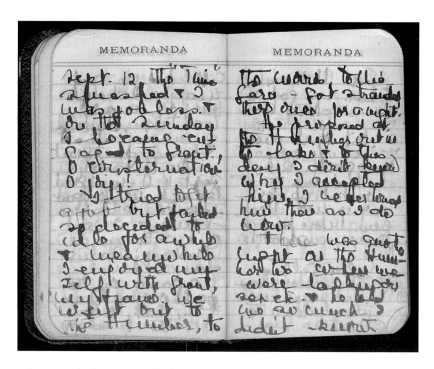

Diary record of a memorable day: September 12, 1919.

CHAPTER 2

On the Road

The end of the First World War brought enormous changes to all Canadians' lives and Gilean Douglas was swept along with the rest. Being a determined young woman without parents but with financial prospects made her simultaneously vulnerable and free. She might be prey to those who would try to capitalize on her assets, yet she had choices that many of her female peers did not.

While not without family—indeed, there were several aunts, uncles, and cousins—she was a loner, an only child who had lived in her own world of actuality and imagination and who was very accustomed to getting her own way. The worlds of business and journalism had already acknowledged her potential and the war had thrown her into contact with people and places far from the enclaves of moneyed Toronto.

After the physical and emotional devastation of the war, the mood became frivolous. Hemlines went up, hair was bobbed, and young people were looking for gaiety and good times. Gilean had the wits, the desire, and the wherewithal to join the party, and separation from her relatives after the disastrous Woodstock sojourn meant there was little in the external world to hold her back. She had been intensely religious before the war, but her internal spiritual world had also changed.

> I couldn't understand how God—a God of love—could ever allow such things to happen, and then when clergymen called for bloodshed and vengeance in their pulpits and religious people applauded them, it seemed to be against everything that I had been taught. . . . I got so I couldn't stand what to me was the hypocrisy of the church. I could never see why people had to go into a stuffy

Slim (right) at Niagara Falls, 1921.

*Photographs and
commentary from
Douglas's
travel journals*

*August 6, 1922—
"Got rightfully reckless today
& each bought
a pair of high leather boots
—perfect wonders!
Feel terribly 'swell'!"*

September 20, 1923—"Lots of mud on road to Estelline! Could only make slow going. Slim fell in mud hole trying to push Lizzie out!"

Camp with Lizzie.

June 3, 1922—"In the aft. dressed up in knickers & went up town. How the natives stared! I must have been the knickered original!"

Slim, Mutt, and Lizzie on bridge.

June 11, 1922—"Campers greatly amused at Slim helping with washing & cooking! Crazy idiots!"

June 22, 1923—"Met some Canadians—7 of 'em in one poor Lizzie!—from Alberta. They came over to see our tires and we had quite a chat. We did some work on their car in evening."

Bobs in stagecoach in Oregon, 1923.

Umatilla Indian Chief in Oregon.

Movie set, Hollywood.

*Hollywood lasso artist
"The Texas Wonder."*

*Movie extras
dressed as Bedouins.*

*October 12, 1922—
"Lizzie's rear-end broke
going up camp hill—
we were nearly dashed
to bottom. Worked in
garage on her half of
night—Charlie!—
all thought me a boy!"*

"Pipe of Peace"—Bobs smoking a pipe, seated on a raft in Yellowstone Park, 1923.

building to worship anyway, when there was the sun and the clean wind outside and when Christ had always seemed to prefer the fields to the temples.[1]

The implicit pantheism of this observation was not to be fully developed until years later in her nature writing. Organized religion had little to give her and less to demand, so any constraints on her were not external but personal. Douglas was quite content to throw over family and class and begin to live by her wits and fashion her own future, a stance not often available to young women in the early 1920s. Indeed, it gave her a quality of independence than has become more associated with the later decades of the century, as she herself was to observe in the 1970s.

Was she a feminist, even then? She certainly felt that women could do anything they chose to do and that gender inequities were unfair. She also understood that women must have economic independence, for without it their only alternative was to marry and, as she later put it in a letter to the *Calgary Herald*, "to marry she has to please a man—and men, believe me, do not 'go for' intelligent women."[2]

On the other hand, she fiercely desired someone for whom she would be the absolute centre of existence. Since the loss of her father, she had sought a worthy object of love—but not at the price of independence. Therein lay the rub. To find a mate who would respect her ambitions and needs yet provide a strong and unquestioning love was a tall order. She was willing to trade quite a bit of autonomy for a partner, but having made the trade, she began to chafe under the terms, and hers were never happy or long relationships. She later opined that had she been a man, the conflicts in her personality would have been tolerated and she would have been able to pursue her public career without sacrificing her personal desires. She was probably right.

In the summer of 1921, however, such introspective analysis was not foremost in her mind. She needed to make decisions. After she lost her job, she gravitated back to the Niagara area for the summer to live in a boarding house. She became part of a happy crowd of young people finding their own new ways of living, and among them were engineers working on the Hydro project along the Welland Canal. Through them, she met a fellow named Slim who was also employed by Hydro. His real name was Cecil Rhodes, but he was going under the surname Thomas, which he said was the name of his adoptive parents. He had been born in Britain, as he later told Douglas, "the illegitimate son of an actress and a musician."[3]

Although he was from an entirely different background and environment than Gilean, Slim was a quick study. He had the ability to fit into a crowd and learn appropriate ways of speaking and behaving. Handsome and attentive, he won Gilean's regard and then her heart. She later recounted in *A February Face*: "I stayed there all summer and, by the time I was to go home, I was in love with Slim and just decided to stay on. There didn't seem to be anything to go back for. I just drifted here and there into whatever patch of water I thought looked to be the pleasantest sailing."

They were engaged at Christmas and married on February 17, 1922, in Hamilton, Ontario. Slim agreed to adopt Gilean's surname as his own, a requirement she would impose on two of her four husbands. Was he one of the proverbial gold diggers? Possibly—but in 1922, they were both enchanted with each other for many of the reasons that drive relationships, not the least of which may be financial. In their case, the potential for wealth was on her side.

The young couple had no pressing demands other than their own amusement, and in due course, they decided to acquire a car and travel around together. They bought a Tin Lizzie, and with enough money to survive, they headed for the romantic west—and south, and east, and north. Slim, a mechanic, had the skills to keep the car on the roads, such as they were. Gilean, going under the nickname "Bobs," delighted in this new free and open life and, with her short hair concealed under a cap and wearing jodhpurs and riding boots, was amused at being taken for a boy.

GYPSY WEATHER

Spring wind and a mackerel sky
Make gypsy weather;
Make heartlit roads where you and I
Shall walk together.
Make heartlit roads where you and I
Find a young spring wind with a mackerel sky,
And far green hills where young dreams lie
In gypsy weather.

Two of us and a love song's flight
Make gypsy weather;
Our feet in tune and our eyes as bright
As a bluebird's feather.
Our feet in tune and our eyes as bright
As the stars that glow in the tender night
For two of us and a love song's flight—
In gypsy weather.[4]

They were having the time of their lives. They took their time, staying at the "tourist camps" that were just becoming common. If they found a place they liked, they stayed for several days or several weeks. Slim helped with housekeeping chores, and Bobs helped with the constant maintenance that Lizzie required. They entered the United States at Buffalo in May 1922. Their route took them south of the Great Lakes and over the plains to Yellowstone Park in Wyoming, where they spent ten weeks before continuing down through Utah and Nevada to Los Angeles.

As they went, Douglas recorded their travels in a journal and with photographs. She had been taking pictures since receiving a camera as a young girl and was becoming a fairly accomplished photographer. Although fun was always the main agenda, she was aware she was training her mind and storing up material that would be of later use in her career.

Slim and Bobs reached California at the end of October 1922 and settled for the next five months in a cottage in Manhattan Beach near Los Angeles. The movie industry was in its first flowering, and the Douglases were among those seduced by the silver screen. They visited movie sets, which Gilean photographed, and she learned what she could of filmmaking, a skill she would later use for educational projects. She was writing and selling freelance articles during this period, and even Slim turned his hand to writing short stories.

In April 1923, they left their Los Angeles cottage for another extended road trip. After spending a couple of weeks picking fruit in California's Sonoma county, they made a long loop northward through Oregon, southward back to Yellowstone, then east to Chicago and down through Missouri, Arkansas, and Texas into the southwestern U.S. They

Christmas Day at the Manhattan Beach cottage, 1922.

Adobe ovens at the San Juan pueblo.

*"A government office building in Santa Fe,
showing the rounded Pueblo architecture."*

*Museum of Art
Santa Fe.*

*Old mission church at
Rancho Del Taos.*

Hermit's Rest at the Grand Canyon.

Refreshment station in the desert.

travelled to Arizona and New Mexico and, like many before and since, found pueblo life fascinating.

"The Romance of New Mexico" is an excellent example of Douglas's early journalism. Drawn from her road trip with Slim and illustrated with her own photographs, she capitalizes on the mystique of the southwest in this article from the February 1926 issue of *Motor Camper & Tourist*, a magazine that catered to an audience travelling in the ever more popular automobile.

THE ROMANCE OF NEW MEXICO
A LAND OF UNUSUAL INTEREST FOR THE MOTOR CAMPER

The highways of New Mexico run not only through a land of interest and of beauty but back through "the pages of unrecorded time." Their dust is the dust of history. Indians dwell beside them in the pueblos of their ancestors. The bells of Spanish missions, built hundreds of years ago, still call the worshippers to prayer. Mexicans live primitively in their adobe houses, while above them loom great snow-capped ranges where wolves, bears, and mountain lions still roam.

My first glimpse of New Mexico was at Texline, Texas, on the Colorado-to-Gulf highway. The even road wound quietly enough through vast prairie lands and gave no hint of the rich store of wonders to which it would soon lead us. At Clayton, a sign informed us that this was the smallest town in the world with a Rotary Club. We—my partner and I—camped there one night and found it a friendly little place with ample camping space on the prairie, boasting some conveniences.

In the sparkling chill of the early morning, we set out for Raton. At Capulin, we climbed Capulin Mountain, a splendid example of extinct volcano, and viewed with expectant hearts the country spread before us. This mountain has an altitude of eight thousand feet, rising fifteen hundred feet above the plain in striking contrast to the general flatness of the surrounding country. Nearby, numerous blister cones—blocks of lava originally blown out by hot air within—held our interest for some little time. Then on to Raton, just thirty miles away.

Raton is an intriguing mixture of sleepiness and efficiency, of modern architecture and Mexican adobes. The Raton range, at the foot of which it lies, seemed to beckon us majestically forward, so, leaving the town, we climbed the wide and well-graded road to the summit where the state line into Colorado is crossed. Great mountain ranges were always in view. We glimpsed the splendid Sangre de Christo mountains, their crests haloed with perpetual snow, and Fisher's Peak, the highest point in the Raton range. We spent the afternoon in Trinidad.

At dusk, on the winding grade of the descent into Raton, we saw the welcoming lights of that little city gleaming far below us where once glowed the campfires of Indians and of pioneers. That night, we passed by the mediocre and very hilly city campground and stayed instead at a small, but level, camp attached to a garage on the Santa Fe Trail.

Our leisurely start next morning, after considerable car repair work, was uneventful. Ten miles out on the Santa Fe Trail, the road divided—the left branch leading to Las Vegas and the right to Taos. We chose the latter, and thereby obtained our passport to Adventure! At first, the road led through gently rolling country and then through cool canyons of green beauty. Gradually, the way grew rougher and steeper, and mountains began to loom around us. The sky became overcast with clouds. We topped Eagle's Nest Pass and marvelled at the silver beauty of Eagle's Nest Lake spread far below. Then we glided down and entered deep forests. From the time we had made the turning near Raton, we had seen only two cars upon the road, both local.

The silence of the mountain woods was only broken by the sound of our own motor, the crackling of branches, and the distant rumble of thunder. As we began the steep ascent to the top of Palo Flechado Pass, the rain began to fall, and we offered up a silent prayer that we would be able to reach the summit before the clay roads became impassable. Our prayer was answered, but by the time our goal was achieved, the rain was falling in torrents and the lightning was flashing its jagged way closer and closer.

I believe I shall always feel, in memory, the thrill of that downward descent. We had no chains, the grade was steep and the road like glass in slipperiness, although lacking its smoothness. Our brakes became coated with mud and water and would hardly grip. We were cold and wet, and night was almost upon us in the mountains, but our hearts still held the thrill of the adventure. Suddenly, a turn brought us in sight of a clearing and, on a rise at the side of the road, an adobe house.

On the house was a rustic sign which read: "Welcome to Shady Brook Inn." We looked longingly at that little wayside hostelry, but Taos was only about ten miles distant and we felt that it was our logical stopping place. Then we started to navigate a sharp turn. Our back wheels skidded, and we found ourselves hanging perilously on the edge of a steep gully! Fortunately, we continued to hang.

"Dad" Bathlot, the proprietor of the inn, appeared on the scene, and in a short time, we were headed back to the Shady Brook Inn. The road to Taos, we were told, was narrow and rough and would have been made absolutely impassable by the rain. We would be taking grave risks if we attempted it that night. One of the best suppers I have ever eaten, a chat around the warm stove and, finally, a comfortable bed, ended our day. Our adventures in this land of romance and beauty had begun.

It rained practically all night, but by morning, the sun was shining brightly and the crisp mountain air made one feel like running and shouting for sheer joy. In front of the inn, on the opposite side of the road, was the Bathlots' garden planted in virgin soil, with bigger cabbages than I have ever seen and many other kinds of vegetables. To the right was a little campground containing a well of mineral water, which they called "The Well of Life" because it had given them back their health. On every side rose the great Sangre de Christo Mountains with the yellow of quivering aspen like sunlight on their wooded slopes. The Bathlots—"Mother" and "Dad" and their two children—are the only Americans for many miles around, the other inhabitants of the mountains being Mexicans and Indians.

Hardly had we finished breakfast when there were wild whoops outside and a bunch of cowboys came down the pass driving a herd of mountain cattle. We had some wonderful exhibits of riding and lassoing before they passed out of sight on their way to Taos.

Armed with a big game rifle belonging to "Dad" and some lunch put up by "Mother," we set out for a day's climbing in the mountains. We followed an old Indian trail and found one tree with initials carved over fifty years ago and another on which the date was 1851, but the letters of the name were practically illegible. On both trees, the bark had grown out and ridged in the form of the letters and figures. We enjoyed a late lunch at the summit and then started down again. The scenery was glorious. Pines and Douglas firs towered above us, and the woods seemed like a vast temple of silent worship.

Halfway down, I saw something dark lying in a hollow by a dead log and went over to investigate it. It sprang erect and dashed into the woods, but not before I had seen that it was a young mountain lion! We must have come up to windward of it and been upon it before it could flee, so it had hidden by the log in hopes that we would pass by without seeing it. That is the only explanation I have of its presence there.

The wild game animals of these mountains at this point are protected by law, but few people travel far from the main roads without a rifle of some sort. The year we were there, one man was killed by a grizzly and another by a mountain lion. That night, we heard the howling of wolves. Coming out upon the porch, I saw upon a rocky ledge, outlined against the sky in the light of the full moon and the stars, the figure of a lone wolf giving his blood-curdling cry of the wild.

The roads were still in bad condition the next day, but we made Taos in good time. We spent an absorbing three days in the little town where the old home of Kit Carson still stands and where he and his wife, Josepha, are buried. In Taos, the great scout lived for many years; in Taos, he was married, and in Taos, he died. No matter where his wanderings carried him, he always returned to this little village of Indians and Mexicans. Also in the cemetery is a monument to the memory of officers and soldiers killed by the Mexicans and Indians near Taos in the conflicts of 1847 and 1854. One of these officers was General Bent, Governor of the State and friend of Kit Carson's, who was massacred by the Pueblos.

The Indians are the most interesting inhabitants of Taos. They occupy two large pueblos in exactly the manner of three centuries ago. Their houses are built of adobe, tier upon tier, with ladders connecting one with another. For cooking, curious conical outdoor ovens are used, built of adobe and probably copied from the Spaniards. At intervals during the year, these Pueblo Indians take part in fiestas which include a mystery play and many dances of war and peace, each one with its special significance to the Indian participators and watchers. But it would require a book to tell of the history, customs, and present life of the Pueblos—and my space is limited. Unfortunately, also, the old chief of the Pueblos at Taos made us promise that we would take no pictures while there. He was most courteous, however, and when we left, we felt like veritable mines of Pueblo information.

The Penitentes, a religious sect, also live at Taos. Each year, they make a pilgrimage, barefooted and clad in rough garments, each carrying a heavy cross upon their shoulders. It is said that they used to crucify one of their number annually, but the secrets of their religion are very closely guarded. A very large art colony is also situated there, and many paintings done by its members are to be seen in the museums of Santa Fe. There are two camp grounds in Taos, one on the outskirts and one in the centre of the town. We chose the latter and, although it lacked most conveniences, we managed to make ourselves very comfortable during our stay.

It is not a hundred miles from Taos to Santa Fe, but the road is both rough and narrow with stretches of heavy sand and some rather bad washouts. However, most of it was under repair when we passed through, so by this time, it should be considerably improved. From a high promontory, with a sheer cliff rising on one side and an equally sheer drop on the other, we glimpsed the Rio Grande River and stood awed by the wild grandeur of the scene. At that point and time of year, the Rio Grande was only a stream running between bare frowning canyon walls as far as an eye can see. Farther south, it becomes a mighty river and, at times, a raging flood. . . .

But, at last, we set our faces definitely toward Albuquerque and the west. On the way we picked up a San Domingo Indian. With him on the running board, we descended La Bajada grade—with its eighteen hairpin turns on a 30 percent grade!—and soon arrived at his native village. Here we were immediately surrounded by curious Indians, and I was made the recipient of a gift of pottery. These Indians have a number of ceremonial dances throughout the year of which the Corn Dance is the principal one. The dancers are all dressed in gala attire, and the dancing is accompanied by drum or tom-tom and the singing of tribal songs.

Between San Domingo and Albuquerque, we passed the Sandia Pueblo village and several Mexican settlements. Perhaps nothing takes one back so many centuries as the ancient method of threshing wheat employed by many Mexicans in this locality. The wheat is brought in from the field, and part of it is scattered around. Goats are then driven over in a circle to trample it down, while from time to time, more grain is thrown on the ground. When the threshing is over, the winnowing is done in the old primitive way. Goats, drawing home-made carts, may also be seen hauling wood down from the surrounding mountains.

When we drove on to the paved streets of Albuquerque, I felt like closing my eyes lest the spell of the past be broken. . . .[5]

The Douglases—Slim and Bobs—settled down again for the winter in Manhattan Beach outside Los Angeles. Life was apparently still lots of fun, but in the spring of 1924, Gilean's thyroid began to act up again and a course of X-ray treatments was needed. With that over, the pair left California for a trip through the southern U.S. By May, they had traversed the southwestern states and arrived in Louisiana—but in New Orleans, Gilean's health again collapsed.

Although I didn't realize then what they were, I was showing all the symptoms of toxic goitre in full force. I was very irritable and emotionally excitable. I perspired excessively, had a rapid pulse and a hot skin. I felt weak in my muscles and my hands trembled, particularly if the fingers happened to be spread out. . . . One day soon afterward, I went into a series of faints when having a tooth extracted and was rushed to hospital. That night, I came close to death.[6]

Part of the crisis was the strain that the enlarged thyroid had placed on her heart. She was to suffer from heart complaints for the rest of her life, but the immediate problem was to devise a way to treat her without further jeopardizing her. Before anything could be done, she was kept in hospital for a month. She had to rest and rebuild her strength before major surgery could be attempted.

Excision was the only known treatment at the time, and two operations were needed to reduce the overactivity of the thyroid gland. In the first, part of the thyroid was tied off to reduce it; in the second, the weakened section was removed. "I almost didn't pull through that second operation," she wrote, "and when I did, I found that I couldn't speak [because of damage to the vocal cords]. For weeks, I had to carry on conversations on slips of paper, but after about three months, my voice came back again—not as strong or as untiring a voice as before and definitely husky, but adequate."[7]

Before the whole episode was over, Gilean spent almost seven months in the New Orleans hospital. When she was finally well enough to leave, Bobs and Slim once again took to the road, but the marriage was in crisis. The amusing agenda of travel and fun had been thoroughly interrupted. Slim was attentive during her stay in hospital and travelled with her to Florida, but their relationship was collapsing. They rented an apartment in Pablo Beach but soon went their separate ways. From her point of view—and it is the only one that remains— Slim deserted her. She left the south in early spring of 1925 and visited relatives in Toledo, Ohio. When she returned to Canada in April, she was still married to Slim—but in fact was once again a single woman.

Entry from Douglas's road trip journal.

CHAPTER 3

The Wandering Years

*B*ack in Toronto in the spring of 1925, Gilean Douglas was on her own again. She rented a flat, bought a new car, and took up life where she had left off before her marriage, supporting herself through journalism. Soon, though, she realized she was cut off from the friends of her childhood. Now young marrieds who had stayed in their class, they had little common ground with a single, separated woman making her way as a journalist. Still, in spite of this, and in spite of continued ill health in the aftermath of her goitre operation, Douglas started a dizzying round of working and socializing.

Between 1926 and 1928, she took several trips through the Great Lakes to do research for articles on shipping conditions on the big freighters. On these trips she became acquainted with ships' officers and radio operators, who became part of her social circle. She began corresponding with several of them and most of them fell under her spell. "You have a fatal attraction Gilean, it seems that most men who come into close contact with you, sooner or later fall in love—in his own particular way—with you," one of them wrote to her in 1928.[1] Another correspondent, Betty Rittenhouse, wrote to Gilean in January of 1928: "So this is another New Beau. My goodness Jill! Where under creation do you pick them up? Here's both Mildred and I dying slowly by inches "old Maids," haven't you some Cast Offs you could patch up and send over to us."[2]

To keep the financial wolves from the door, Douglas was turning out all kinds of journalism and using a myriad of pseudonyms. In part these pen names helped her to be published but in part they also gave her different identities for different kinds of writing. The benefit of assuming a new identity through a new name was that it opened up different types of expression and different subject matter. In addition, she was handling the problem of bias against women writers by using a male name—a venerable solution to the problem women faced getting published.

Even her own unusual name led some people to think she was a man. One correspondent, Flossie Faith, not only took Gilean for a man but fantasized a whole relationship with "him." Gilean did not disabuse Flossie of this misunderstanding despite a correspondence of several years. Douglas also used female pen names under which to submit articles, particularly to journals aimed at a female audience. If work was not accepted under one name, she would often use another and resubmit—sometimes to the same journal!

Although Douglas was having to hustle to make ends meet as a "scribbling woman," she was becoming more serious about her creative writing and was beginning to receive recognition as a poet. She maintained her connections to other writers and joined several writers' organizations, such as the National League of Pen Women. Such connections would prove fruitful; she received an annual stipend from the Canadian Writers' Federation for many years in her later life.

Through the latter part of the 1920s, Douglas worked hard as a writer but always found time for leisure pursuits as well. She spent many weeks in northern Ontario enjoying camping, hunting, canoeing, and skiing vacations with her group of friends. Aviation was becoming popular, and Douglas took lessons and learned to pilot an airplane.

Travel remained an important part of her life and she made many trips through Canada and the States. Always observant and with her writing in mind, she gathered photographs and information on all these journeys. One of her favourite places was the desert, and she stayed in Reno, Nevada from October 1928 to March 1929. There she continued her writing career and played an active part in community organizations such as the Reno Business Girls Club and the YWCA. She also turned her movie knowledge to good advantage by landing a contract to create educational films for the New York State Board of Education.

SIERRA SONG

Looking down from the rim of heaven
I see blue-eyed morning swing
on golden ropes over valley darkness—
out and down until everything
is drenched with light and the brown hills waken,
flushed from sleep, to flash of wing.

Looking down from the rim of heaven
cities small as a gossiped word
lie at my feet, with their strident yammer
only a light tale I have heard
that lost itself in the manzanita
and the song of a white-crowned bird.

Looking down from the rim of heaven
with the stars in my moon-gilt hair,
I am caught by the hand of silence
and held for a shining moment where
the old is new and the truth forgotten
waits in the tingling darkness there.[3]

Throughout these years, she conquered many hearts although her own still sought the perfect mate.

> So the merry-go-round began again: working too hard, playing too long, always on the defensive and under strain. I neither drank nor smoked nor was I promiscuous, except with kisses. But I went out with almost any man who asked me and finally, when the sense of homelessness became more than I could bear, I married again. This desperate feeling of wanting to belong, which was always with me, blinded me to the true character of the men I met. I saw them as I wanted them to be: almost perfect beings who would give me a home, security, love—all those things I had wanted so much for so long.[4]

Her sense of desperation led her to enter a marriage with Charles Norman Haldenby on July 27, 1929, in Toronto. There is little evidence of this marriage in Douglas's papers: a few references in her writings to four marriages, a mention of the name "Norman," several letters and photographs. No journal entries or letters explain the circumstances of this marriage and almost the only concrete information about it comes from a copy of the marriage certificate obtained from the Department of Vital Statistics in Ontario (there was no copy among Douglas's papers). Gilean did, however, tell a Vancouver friend about the circumstances surrounding the end of the marriage.

Haldenby, a bond salesman, was clearly from a different background than Douglas's first husband, and the wedding took place at St. Thomas Church with the groom's mother and the bride's aunt as witnesses. Douglas gave her status as "spinster" and there is no indication of her previous marriage, which had not been dissolved. However, she apparently thought Slim was dead for she had heard nothing of him other than rumours he had died in Mexico. The revelation to the contrary came in a spectacular public disclosure not long after Douglas and Haldenby were married. The newlyweds were at a dance at a Toronto hotel when in walked Slim, looking for his wife. Haldenby left on the spot. Douglas's second "marriage" was over, and she apparently never saw Haldenby again.

No diaries and few letters survive from the period between 1929 and 1933. Douglas presumably returned to her life as a single working woman, but two failed marriages did not discourage her ongoing search for the right man. By 1933, she was planning another marriage. Her third husband-to-be, Eric Altherr, was a chemical engineer working for Buffalo Ankerite Mines in Northern Ontario. Born in Switzerland, educated and urbane, he seemed to be the ideal partner she had sought. This wedding had the approval of her family and the engagement was officially announced by her cousin and his wife, Sir Henry and Lady Drayton of Ottawa. This time, Gilean, who was still married to Slim, travelled to Reno, Nevada and obtained a divorce from him on the grounds of desertion for longer than five years. Although she had seen Slim in California in 1927 and at the fateful meeting in Toronto, they had not lived together after their separation in 1925. The divorce went uncontested. Indeed, it is doubtful that Slim even knew it was happening, since Gilean gave his address as the apartment they had shared in 1925 in Florida. The summons was sent there and never acknowledged.

Since Douglas had resided in Reno during the twenties, she had a circle of friends who feted the upcoming marriage in a traditional bridal shower. The wedding took place in Chicago, but even then her emotions were mixed. In a post-nuptial agreement, the newlyweds granted each other "full control of their own separate property, both real and personal, to lease, sell, and dispose of the same and receive all moneys, rents, issues, and profits thereof without molestation from the other, renouncing forever all claims in law and in equity, of curtesy, dower, homestead, and survivorship."[5] She wasn't a young, blushing bride and had learned the hard way of the necessity for economic independence in an emotional involvement.

Despite this forethought, the preparations for and expectations of the marriage proved to be more satisfying than the relationship itself. The Altherrs were married in Chicago in late August of 1933 and spent their honeymoon at the Chicago World's Fair. There were signs of trouble almost immediately. Douglas's journal reveals that she spent January of 1934 by herself, but it hints at a reconciliation taking place in February. Unfortunately, it seemed that Eric was not the perfect mate she was seeking.

> Women were his weakness and he couldn't leave them alone. Almost from the start I was in turmoil of jealousy and despair. Hyperthyroid symptoms—which had never been entirely absent—began to flare up again and shortly after I became pregnant I found myself with another toxic goitre. I lost my baby . . . and finally I found myself back in hospital.[6]

The miscarriage occurred in the spring of 1934. Her friend Louise Meginness was shocked to hear the news. "I am truly sorry to hear of all your misfortunes. . . . I could never imagine you in the role of a mother, but if you really want to be one you can try again perhaps."[7] However, the consequence of this miscarriage was that Gilean Douglas would never be able to have children. She did have an affinity for children, and they for her, but her most profound maternal inclinations would be directed toward nature.

Although she remained married to Eric and lived with him off and on for three years before the final break, the relationship never had much success and the couple was often apart. She maintained an apartment in Toronto between travels, while his work kept him in

Timmins. Although she was in many respects living the life of an independent woman, there was enough mutual commitment that the couple decided to build a house in Timmins. As was often the case for Douglas, planning and correspondence were the most satisfactory aspects of the relationship. After many letters and decisions, the house became a reality, but the marriage foundered.

In 1937, the Altherrs separated as both parties had become involved with other people. Although Gilean's experiences with marriage had proved unhappy, she was still looking for a man who could assuage her sense of homelessness. She fell in love again, this time with Ted Geppert, a colleague of Eric's at the Buffalo Ankerite mine. Since both were married, they could not wed immediately but made plans to begin a new life together on the West Coast.

In spite of her marital problems, the thirties were fruitful years for Douglas's writing. Her freelance work was selling well and she was enjoying increasing success with her poetry, which often reflected her great desire for love and explored the themes of unrequited love and rejection.

WHEN APRIL

When April snow is falling
I'll feel the chill of pain
Come sharply, come relentlessly,
And I shall hear the rain
Of autumn tapping on a roof
Where leaved winds blew
When love sat by the birch flame with
My heart and you.

When winter stars are shining
I shall not see the sky,
But all the waters and the woods
Where careless you and I
Went wandering and singing
While gold leaves fell
Will be as clear as heaven
And as bright as hell.[8]

Often her journalism reflected ideas on the "woman question" and her dissatisfaction with the way marriage was organized. Some of these articles later appeared as the work of Grant Madison, and Douglas, presumably with tongue in cheek, used her male persona to argue passionately for the rights of women. Although Gilean Douglas used many pseudonyms over the course of her life, Grant Madison was one of her favourites. The given name was that of her first serious boyfriend, and the surname was the street of her birth. The name was used primarily for her outdoor writing, but she often used it for correspondence as well. This, and Gilean's own ambiguous given name, sometimes led readers to assume she was a man—a perception she often let stand.

"Can You Marry and Live?" is one of Douglas's articles on the conditions faced by women. It was submitted as the work of Grant Madison, a "manly man" who published outdoor articles but still had a sense of fair play for the opposite sex.

CAN YOU MARRY AND LIVE?

I wonder if marriage could ever have come into existence without us first destroying that urgent sense of life with which we are all born? That vital feeling of being part of the great universe is quietly killed in each generation until now it barely survives childhood. Men are more likely to retain it than women for they are never thrust quite so violently into the mould of civilization. Civilization and marriage as we know it are, of course, inseparable.

It may seem odd to speak of something which should be fulfillment and joy as being without life, but remember that I am speaking of marriage and not just of mating. I am speaking of the necessity to live, eat, and sleep with someone until death do you part. Of not being able to escape from their society, when work is done, without being worried about or upbraided. Of not, except in working hours, being able to talk with someone of the opposite sex except in the presence of your spouse. Of waking up in the morning with the knowledge that here is another day of questions to be answered, of conversation to be made. Of going to bed at night with the breathing of that other person to remind you that there is no escape from them, except fleetingly in sleep.

I realize that I am walking a tightrope here because most people are quite sure that when you speak of freedom in reference to marriage you really mean license. But I don't. I mean that freedom to live up to the very highest peak in you. The freedom to think for yourself and to act from that thinking. The blessed freedom to be alone when you want to, even if that aloneness is found best in a crowd of strangers.

*Return to
Toronto, 1925.*

Douglas with her new car, 1925.

*Outdoor life:
Douglas in
Northern Ontario,
1925–1930.*

"The day I soloed!"

Douglas's second husband, Norman Haldenby, 1929.

*Douglas seated on porch of house she shared
with Eric Altherr in Timmins, Ontario, c. 1934.*

Skiing.

Always the camera!

No other relationship is so coercing as marriage, as the statistics on deserting husbands certainly illustrate. Brother and sister, parent and child or best friends are not expected to be inseparable. There is always the privilege of leaving the other without scandal and you can pawn a loaf of bread for a hyacinth without being made to feel either a fool or a rascal.

In marriage the greater the love and the better the man the stronger are the bonds. I am dealing with men in this argument for the situation of women is so much worse that I doubt my ability to deal with it at all. But perhaps that's the way women like things to be? To make me believe that you must erase from my mind the numbers of women who desert even their children in order to get away from intolerable situations; of women sitting at dark windows while their husbands sleep behind them; of women in those "perfect" marriages with that look of quiet desperation behind their acquiescent eyes.

What, too, of the drunkenness or adultery or brutality which feature so many marriages? What are one or both trying to escape from and what are they trying to find? What of the physical and mental illnesses and the incessant clamour for speed—as though one could, perhaps, outrun one's shadow? I notice that there is supposed to be no "giving in marriage" in heaven and I wonder how many of us want to go there for just that reason.

It isn't that you should trade your present wife off for another one, because that wouldn't help matters in the least. It is just that you want to wake up in the morning with that upsurge of joy because the day is yours, without nagging or question or demanding love. You were born one certain person with special abilities and characteristics; you want to bring those characteristics and abilities to their fullest and best fruition. But how is that possible when you are teamed so closely with someone who goes either faster or slower than you do, who trips you with their mistakes or rings your nose with their perfections? You can adjust, of course, but beyond a certain point of adjustment there is nothing left of you.

I doubt if it was ever meant that two people should be shackled so tightly. A man speaks of his wife as "the ball and chain"; a woman refers to her husband as "the lord and master." Perhaps they laugh about it, but they have said it truly. They say too: "Oh, well, that's life." But is it really? It is civilization, but it isn't life. It is existence as we have made it, but it isn't life. No one was ever born with the soul of a slave, but matrimony has helped us to arrive at that condition.

How much of our present desire to be state-owned and operated can be traced to the indoctrination of marriage? It abhors solitude and stultifies originality. It has pounded us with such words as duty, sacrifice, sanctity until we are blind and lame and disfigured. Nothing is finer than those words if we know what they really mean and when and how they should be used. But when the good bread of them has been turned into stones then they become only our hurt and not our sustenance.

Is there no way that we can marry and yet live? Only when love is not interpreted as possessiveness; only when desire to be a distinct personality is not construed as neglect; only when people mind their own business and leave their neighbours' alone. Only when the world's moulds are changed to fit that which is best and highest in us.[9]

Despite her intellectual dissections of marriage and all its problems, Douglas was still seeking that one man who could assuage her sense of homelessness. She hoped her relationship with Ted Geppert would satisfy this perpetual longing.

Ted Geppert, 1939.

CHAPTER 4

The Mountains: Paradise Found

*T*he years between 1937 and 1947 were the worst of times and the best of times. Along with all of the citizens of the Allied countries, Gilean Douglas looked in horror at the progress of the Second World War. Having lived through the first war, she despaired at the return of such global conflagration. Always one to approach all friends and strangers with equity, Douglas was appalled by the racial theories of Hitler. She knew what it was to be the outsider shunned by superior insiders and she felt the threat of Nazism keenly.

SONG AGAINST HATE

Hate will dull the eye's shine,
Hate will draw the mouth thin
And all that was mine,
Without and within,
Will go spilled like wine.

Then no one will tell us that there are rivers,
That there are rivers of cool mountain water
(For who will remember the green mountain
places?)
And that the forests are deep and shadowy
With birds making music in them forever.

The sword will not turn into a ploughshare
Or the sharp spears into pruning hooks
(For who will remember the green places?)
When God has been crucified again upon hate
And poets have died sorrowing for beauty.[1]

Closer to home, her personal life was once again in turmoil, and as always, bad health followed close on the heels of emotional stress. Douglas and Geppert had moved to Vancouver in 1938, when he took a course in placer mining in order to prepare for prospecting in the Cascade Mountains near Hope, British Columbia. While Ted was becoming established, Gilean continued to travel and write. She made frequent trips back to Ontario but she gave up her Toronto apartment, finalized her divorce from Eric Altherr, and moved permanently to the West Coast. This area of the continent had always appealed to her and had often been her temporary home, but now her move was final and she would spend the rest of her life in British Columbia.

The relationship between Douglas and Geppert flourished while they were apart and keeping each other in reach through letters, but their time together was often marked by disagreements. In addition, Geppert, a naturalized Canadian of German background, had his movements restricted. Had Douglas married him, she too would have had to report her whereabouts to authorities. Her autobiography, *A February Face*, was begun at the nadir of despair in her early forties.

WHEN I LOOK BACK

When I look back on the fields I've sown,
The weedy prose and the spindling rhyme,
I know again what I've always known;
So much to do and so little time.

The seasons lean on my sweated shoulder;
Before there is green through the heavy clay
The year is old and I am older
And now is already yesterday.

I visioned acres of golden earing
And ripened fruits of a fertile loam;
But it is fall in my thistled clearing
And I have nothing for harvest home.[2]

Her marriage to Altherr over and her relationship with Geppert floundering, Douglas looked back on her life to that point as a series of failures and on herself as a gullible fool. Yet, she still confided to her diary that "I am glad my life has been eventful and not drab—and so correct! Pain and joy are the same thing."[3]

Despite this welcoming of a life lived intensely, her health was precarious and she was being advised to have another thyroid operation. She refused, though she was told that without the operation she would face the possibility of cancer and the certainty of a further weakened heart. As if her health worries weren't enough, she was under financial duress because of the war. Yet at this time of crisis, she found the real solution to her desire for home—in a place rather than a relationship.

In 1939, Gilean visited Ted at his cabin in the mountains northeast of Hope, British Columbia, along the Coquihalla River. She recognized immediately that this would become her own home.

> Always in the back of my mind was the desire for that one perfect place where I could feel fulfilled and truly at home. I found it. I knew I had—the moment I entered the mountain-fenced valley and saw the silvery shake roof of a cabin trying to peer at me over fireweed and salmonberry brush.[4]

Always described in terms befitting a beloved, the cabin and its natural setting were to replace the striving "to come first with someone again."[5] Nature, particularly the mountains around her, became the lover that would grant her the stability and peace she had sought in all her relationships.

> If we still praise tall mountains and the sky
> It is because there is need to know
> That, in the darkly sanguine ebb and flow
> With reason lashed upon the spar of why,
> Here is serenity: men war and die,
> Yet peace remains. The frail years come and go,
> But here is calm and certainty that no
> Mad mouth of greed can shame or terrify.[6]

Two of her collections of nature writing, *Silence Is My Homeland*, and *River for My Sidewalk*, recollect the years Douglas spent in the mountains between 1939 and 1947. While she continued to travel and to work as a journalist, more and more her life centred around the cabin and the surrounding environment. Protective of the solitude of her mountain home, she was careful not to reveal its exact location in any of her writings. Although she described the physical surroundings accurately, and even provided a map in *Silence Is My Homeland*, she always used pseudonyms for the rivers, mountains, and small settlements of the area. Sadly, the Coquihalla highway, which was constructed during the 1980s, now runs close to the property and eliminates the need for any further secrecy.

The cabin sat on a flat bench formed by the meeting of two rivers, the Sowaqua and the Coquihalla. (Douglas referred to them as the Wren and the Teal.) Originally constructed by goldminers, the small building was much in need of refurbishing and repair. Douglas threw herself into the job in a round of cleaning and painting reminiscent of her first apartment in Toronto. Again her desire to domesticate a new space and fill it with the memorabilia of her life was urgent. Throughout her long and peripatetic life, Douglas always brought her old friends—books, letters, and diaries; furniture and housewares. Although many of the more valuable items had to be sacrificed as financial need increased, she always made a home with the mementoes of the past.

The new endeavour in the mountains first required turning the cabin into a home and the land into a garden. Like so many of her most profoundly important undertakings, the garden combined need and desire. She grew food for sustenance, but it was important to her to have a garden that was also aesthetically satisfying. Indeed it is difficult to separate the hungers of the body from those of the spirit. The garden satisfied both, and the years at the cabin introduced her to the pleasures and responsibilities of working the land, as she would for the rest of her long life.

In the poem "Prelude to Peace" from *The Pattern Set*, Douglas expresses her delight: "At last I have found solitude and know / That life without it is a frantic thing." Although Geppert was often with her at the cabin for the next few years, she was also there alone for long periods and the silence and seclusion she experienced answered a need in her. Much of Douglas's poetry and prose are built upon the themes of silence and solitude which also form the foundation for her identity as a person and as a writer. At this point in her life, her concern for nature and love of writing coalesced in a profound personal encounter with the mountains, as expressed in her memoir *Silence Is My Homeland.*

As the mountains became dearer, Gilean's relationship with Ted Geppert grew more distant. It was often more satisfactory in absence than in presence, a sentiment expressed in her poem "The Woman Speaks":

> Now you have gone you are more truly mine
> Than you have been in all the days we shared.
> Here, where we sat, I sit again and say:
> "This thing he touched and that he laid aside;
> This book he read; that letter is from him."
> And, saying this, I see your sudden smile
> And long to kiss the tiny lines that crease
> The corners of your tender, laughing eyes.
>
> But when you come you will be lost to me;
> You will be careless and you will forget
> The little things of love. You will not like
> My verse and I shall hate your ceaseless talk
> Of stocks and loans and muddled politics.
> Of all the words we speak there are but four
> Which we both know and those: "I love you, dear."[7]

First published in 1939, this poem distills a recurring experience in Douglas's life—relationships flourished in distance and letters, but reality often fell short of expectation. In 1941, Gilean purchased the mountain property from Ted for one hundred dollars. As the relationship waned over the next two years, Gilean was more frequently alone in the mountains. By 1943, the liaison was over, and the cabin became her solitary home. However, she continued to travel down to Vancouver to see friends, do research for her writing, and conduct business.

Douglas's writing continued unabated in spite of personal upheaval, and indeed, perhaps her finest writing came from this time. *Silence Is My Homeland* was crafted as one long meditation on a life in the mountains. Organized, as is frequently the case in nature writing, into a calendar of the cycle of life played out against the cycle of nature, the work emphasizes the themes of solitude and silence, the importance of writing, and the search for and finding of home in nature. Locating a publisher for this text was difficult; Douglas faced not only incredulity that the author could be female, but also lack of interest in the ecological themes of the text. Although she did not find a publisher until the mid-seventies when the world had caught up with the environmental and feminist aspects of the text, her vision of finding home in nature was achieved in her life in the mountains. The first chapter of *Silence* records her arrival in the mountains and transforms this experience into the narrative of Paradise Found.

HOME

Let the fields and the gliding streams in the valleys delight me.
Inglorious, let me court the rivers and forests.
VIRGIL

For more than twenty years I had been homeless. It was not that I had no roof over my head during that time, but that I had too many. Roofs of relatives' houses, schools, boarding houses, apartments, duplexes, tents, automobiles, trains, ships, summer cottages. But there had never been a home. I had watered plants in pots and window boxes; I had sprayed other people's roses or dug around dejected annuals in tiny plots beside brick walls. Once there had even been a minute vegetable corner where carrots, radishes and lettuce put up a gallant battle against wornout and undernourished soil. But there had never been a garden. Not a real garden.

Then one day as I was fishing a strange western river, I came to a deep pool where the steelhead and brook trout were both wise and wary. I flicked a red admiral across the dark green water, hoping for a Dolly Varden, and then I looked up at my surroundings. My right arm dropped slowly to my side, and the top of my rod broke the surface of the pool. I stood perfectly still and was not conscious that I breathed, for there, right across from me, gazing into my face with its deep-set windows, was—my home.

A little river bounced down through mountain passes to join, just east of the pool, the larger river I had been following. The little river was the Wren; its companion, the Teal. Together they formed two sides of a rectangle of which the third was a high wooded mountain—very appropriately called Evergreen—and the fourth a forest. Within this rectangle lay a clearing of perhaps two acres with a cabin in the centre and three smaller outbuildings nearby. The whole was a plateau raised some fifty feet above water level and covered with wild berry bushes and large stumps.

"Grant Madison"
—This photo was often used
by Douglas as an illustration for
her mountain articles.

"Cage and cable—the only way
of crossing the Teal River."

"The cage in action."

"Home in the wilderness"—
Douglas's cabin with
Fireweed Mountain in
the background.

First photograph of the
cabin, taken from across the
Coquihalla River. The old
camera scratched the negatives.

*"Part of living-room
and glimpse of bedroom.
I think Old Bill and I
had just come in from
trail clearing."*

*"The little cabin is
warm and cosy."*

"On dark days the valley is dark also."

Douglas standing in her garden.

Ted Geppert packing supplies.

*"Here there is everything I need
for health, wealth and happiness."*

*"The kitchen is cedar-panelled
and bright with sun."*

"Insulated by snow, the heart of my home beats warmly."

"When I first came to the valley. The wire isn't for phone or lights!"

Fording the river below the pool, I went on a reconnaissance tour. Yet I knew before I climbed the short, steep bank to the clearing that this was the house in which I was going to live, that this underbrush was the vegetable field I was going to cultivate. When the heavy nail-studded door of fir swung open upon the musty and dark interior of the cabin, I was already seeing visions. That was, indeed, almost all I could see. There were eleven windows in the three rooms with, by a miracle, only two panes broken, but they were all too grimy to admit more than a mulatto twilight. Everything was incredibly dirty, and the air was high with mould and mouse. The cedar panelling of walls and ceiling was hung with cobweb tapestry and the rough fir floor—there is, unfortunately, no hardwood of any size in the vicinity—looked as if it might be several inches lower when it was scraped and scrubbed.

But in less than half an hour all that was changed. There was a corner bunk in the bedroom with an attached table at the side and book shelves that were built into the foot. A lampstand nestled above in the angle of the wall, with another to balance it in the diagonal corner. A built-in desk and cupboards filled the other corners, while two chairs—already in residence—and a small table under one of the windows completed the furnishings.

The living-room also had a built-in bunk, desk and lampstands. There was a cupboard opposite the stone fireplace and a large bookcase in one of the walls, just where firelight with its pagan art would illuminate the bindings. Butterbox chairs and a drop-leaf table—also in residence and made by better carpenters than my neighbors and I turned out to be—were placed on the dark brown floor covered with hand-hooked rugs; homespun curtains contrasted with the white—or perhaps red—window-trim. Another door, half glass, opened onto a small front porch with a green roof and a gay red floor. And yes—I almost forgot—there was also a new door in the bedroom, opening onto a grassy terrace where summer meals could be flavoured by sun and wind.

The kitchen had a drop-leaf table and several built-in cupboards in addition to the cabinet, stove and water pail table already there. Chinese blue and lacquer red answered the cabin's cry for colour, and gay wooden plaques brightened the satin cedar walls. Outside, my little home looked as though it had sprung from the very soil on which it stood. An eaved green roof contrasted with the reddish tinge of the hemlock bark walls, and blossoming green window boxes pictured themselves against white trim. Bordered stone paths and flowerbeds were everywhere in the clearing, but there was nothing straight or formal—nothing that could not live with the lovely inconsequence of forest, river and mountain.

Yes, after half an hour on that August morning, it was exactly like that. It was—and almost is. But the reality came only after several months and considerable assistance. For I was no carpenter. Neither was I a gardener—although I attended to all that part myself—or anything very much except, perhaps, a writer. I had been accustomed all my life to comfort flowing from gadgets that one pushed or pulled; to electricity, plumbing (of course I *did* have running water—in the rivers) and all the many contraptions—with an accent on the "trap"—which we of this century feel we cannot live without. But I did not miss them. I sloughed off civilization as one doffs a coat that is too tight and found that I had never been so comfortable before.

I will admit, however, that the board situation was a trifle startling to one who had been accustomed to lumber yards at the other end of a telephone. Here you go out and catch a likely looking cedar tree and imitate George Washington. You saw the best parts of it into six-foot lengths and then, with the aid of a froe, a sledge hammer and considerable profanity, you split off shakes—known as boards "outside"—of the desired thickness. One of those unforgettable moments comes when you discover that the interior of your tree has as many waves as a permanent or is as knotty as a rheumatic gaffer. Then you count ten, say it anyway and begin all over.

Of course it is not necessary to cut down a tree when there is a good one on the ground. If it had been, my cabin would have gone shakeless forever. Neither is it necessary to use cedar, but the wood is both light and enduring, great assets when you are transport, sawmill and furniture factory all in one. When you have carried the boards home on your sturdy shoulders, you plane them for hours and hours until they are as smooth as a politician's manner. After that you keep them polished and receive congratulations.

But I had no need of congratulations, for to me those hours of planning [*sic*] and polishing were filled with happiness. Those boards were part of me and of my home as they never could have been if I had bought them from a sawmill. Why, they had grown on my land; they had felt the same cool wind that came down from the uplands in summer. They were related to those very trees that had been felled to build part of my cabin in 1860 and to finish it fifteen years ago. There had been another cabin nearby in the gold-rush days, but it had evidently been wiped out by fire for I discovered the charred foundation logs when I was putting in the big rock garden and steps beside the patch leading downhill to the Teal. Another ancient cabin—a small one of logs—still stands on the other side of the Wren just below Cougar mountain. Most of my good leaf mould has come from there, for erosion and the many deciduous trees have combined to produce a rich soil. But the old prospectors who built the cabin thought even less of comfort than I, for the whole affair is only about the size of my bedroom, with just space enough for a palsied cedar shake bunk, a stool and a small table on which the stove stood, although cooking was also done over a stone fireplace outside. There is no window at all, and the whole gives an impression of a den rather than of a dwelling.

My reconnaissance that first August showed me that my own soil was fairly good, although baked hard by the summer sun. A few gallant sweet williams struggled up through it, and there were enough wild berry bushes to satisfy even the most ardent fruit eater. Of course they needed pruning badly, and in many places the forest was beginning to take its own back again. Some attempt had evidently been made at a vegetable garden at one time, and there were weedy flowerbeds around the house. I have been able to learn very little about those who occupied the cabin before me, but their handiwork tells me that they cared enough to put time and thought and patient craft into it, and for that I am glad. A place that has been loved, even a little, is a good place to live. Loving and living go together.

So that September I moved in. "It is a comfortable feeling to know that you stand on your own ground. Land is about the only thing that can't fly away." The woodshed was half-full of fir, alder, maple, cedar and hemlock, while strawberry plants and wildflowers covered the clearing. I could hardly wait to obey Thoreau and begin to put foundations under my castle in the air. Of my little domain I could feel: "However small it is on the surface, it is four thousand miles deep, and that is a very handsome property."

It was the great moment of my life when I waded the Teal River with my packboard on my back and stood at last on my own ground. I can never describe the feeling that surged up inside me then. I stood now where I should have been always. I felt kinship in everything around me, and the long city years of noise and faces were just fading photographs. What it meant to me to walk in my own door and know that all this was mine—mine—I cannot put in words. I kept touching things: flowers, furniture, even the piled wood as though they were all my children, my children whom I loved very much. My heart sang every moment and I was impatient with sleep.

September and October were golden months. Gradually the slopes of Fireweed—the fire-scarred mountain on the north side of the Teal—and Cougar mountain showed yellow and crimson, and even Evergreen betrayed glowing touches here and there against the steady darkness of its conifers. The days were warm sunshine and the cool nights glinted with silver. The water in the rivers began to rise, but before it was too high for wading I had rejuvenated—again with considerable assistance —the cables across each stream and repaired the cages to ride in. Before the November rains arrived, the woodshed was filled, an acre of land dug over, a fair amount of bush cleared and my roof mended. The larger stumps had to remain, but I partially hollowed them out and filled them with earth for spring flowers.

My pride in everything would have amused an outsider. Between writing, carpentering and warming the house against the snows of that first winter, I worked twelve to fourteen hours a day—and even that workload was not enough to satisfy me. Everything I did was joyful. It was, perhaps, just as well for my life of freedom that no one saw me gloating over my handiwork or going outside to talk to the great Douglas fir which had become my particular friend! I could not explore my domain enough or look too often at the magnificent views that soothed my eyes like sleep. It was impossible to decide which season was the loveliest.

> There is no season such delight can bring,
> As summer, autumn, winter, and the spring.

Watching each season go was like parting from a loved companion, but my sorrow was never too great or I should not have been able to welcome properly the comrade just arriving.

Putting my first seeds into the ground was a revelation. I felt as though the skies had opened and shown me a vision of life as it should be. When I was actually eating my own vegetables and fruits, with my own flowers on the table, I would not have changed places with anyone in the world. How I pitied city people— of whom I had been one such a short time before. With even their air filtered for them, what artificial and sterile lives they led. How could they ever get down to the vital root of things, separated as they were from the good earth by brick and stone? Surely they also were separated from much of the life force and from the curative powers of earth.

So spring, with violets and trilliums flowering in my woods, flowed into summer. The soft, cool air changed to warm winds and rainless dust. I was up at dawn to work among my vegetables and flowers before the sun was on them, and in the evening I would carry up pails from the Wren for watering. It was the following year before ram, tank and troughs were put in to solve the acute irrigation problem.

I discovered that my cabin was close to four east-west and two north-south trails, but that these forest highways were only for pedestrians or pack horses. Everything had to be brought in on human backs or on those of broncos—if one possessed the latter luxury. I had known from the beginning that my nearest neighbor was three miles away and that my only link with "outside" would be the small branch railway that toddled along the slope of Fireweed mountain. My neighbors considered themselves very fortunate that they were so much closer to the railroad than I, while I was delighted that I was so much farther off from it than they. They were convinced that I was very wrong to feel as I did in this matter, while I had no thoughts at all on the subject as it concerned them. There was far too much else to think about that first year. At any time Jeremy Taylor has my full endorsement when he says: "Every man hath in his own life sins enough, in his own mind trouble enough; so that curiositie after the affairs of others cannot be without envy and an evil minde. What is it to me if any Neighbour's Grandfather were a Syrian, or his Grandmother illegitimate, or that another is indebted five thousand pounds, or whether his wife be expensive?"

But when the wind is blowing from the north, it is pleasant to awaken in the night and hear the far-off whistle of the train as it picks its way along the mountainside with a sheer drop of two or three hundred feet below it. There is one engine that is very blasé about it all, and its toots for dangerous curves—of which there are many—are decidedly perfunctory. But when a new engine is on the line, then what wailing and caterwauling! The prairie engines, which are suddenly transferred to this mountain run, practically have nervous breakdowns, and it is quite heartrending to hear their plaintive tootles, which sound as though they were being whipped into going ahead at all.

Most of the forest along the Teal River has been timbered off, but up the Wren fire has been the only devastator as it is too arduous an undertaking to get the logs out and up to the railroad. A shingle mill operated not far away until twelve years ago, and the first sawmill went in at the same time as the gold hunters. Pole cutters have been through at various periods and now there are very few really large trees left standing. On my land, before I came, a fir nearly seven feet in diameter was felled simply for boards and firewood—and three-fourths of it is still lying there. Such signs of vandalism—and there are many of them—make me glad that I could rescue at least a few acres and save such friends as my big Douglas fir (over four hundred years old and with his bark worn off by mountain lions for more than seven feet around the base) from destruction.

I did not learn all these things in that first spring and summer, but I came tentatively to know my immediate surroundings and particularly Home Wood, the fourth side of my rectangle. I also came to know my immediate neighbors: furred, feathered and finned. One summer night I walked out the kitchen door to find Mrs. Barrow's Goldeneye Duck waddling happily up the path from the Wren. She and I became very friendly indeed, and I was glad that I was there to cluck my tongue sympathetically when she told me the sad tale of a husband who spent most of the summer basking at the seaside, leaving her to bring up the family alone.

One of my weekend guests was unusually interesting. I heard that a bird—what kind no one seemed to know—had been shot near the railroad and that its mate was there still—and alive. That was enough. In a very short while he was reposing on my very young front lawn while I tried to examine the injuries I was sure he must have. But Gussie the grebe refused to cooperate. His black crest went up, his eyes shot fire and his beak snapped with plain and angry intent. He had spent at least four days beside the railroad track—well over a mile, by the shortest route, from his native element—with nothing to eat and with the trains thundering by only a few feet away. But his spirit was magnificently intact. If he had injuries, originally, I could detect nothing now. I kept him that Sunday afternoon and night until I was convinced that he had suffered no damage, then I let him go, for it was impossible for me to obtain enough of his favorite foods and, besides, my lawn (or my cabin at night) was definitely no place for such a warrior.

When we came to the river I held Gussie in my hands for a few moments and then placed him on the water. He flashed underneath it and then appeared again several yards away. He floated down toward Dubh Glas, the big pool of Teal River, and held himself there against the current while he looked anxiously upstream. Perhaps he thought that he might find his mate again if he could make his way through that white water. Finally he seemed to make up his mind that she must have gone downstream ahead of him to the larger Mallard River. I watched him until a bend hid him from view and I was sorry to see him go. Gussie was a rare spirit. It would have been pleasant to have had a few words with the man who was so ready with his gun.

So then it was fall again and I had been in my house a year. Asters were blooming in my garden and their wild brothers brightened the hills and river banks. Smoke from my chimney mingled with the blue haze which drifted over forest and mountain while the rivers sang softly in those days before the floods of autumn. Wren and Alaska robin chirped and called; squirrels were very active and noisy. The Canada jays began to prepare for winter, and so did I. Soon the snow would come swirling down the canyon and through the woods and I must be ready for it.

Those woods had seemed a dark, mysterious place in the beginning, but now they were more familiar to me than any street in any city I had ever known—and I had known many. The gravelled paths among my flowers and vegetables were friendly ways also, and even the outland trails were not strange any more. In that second fall the mists of Evergreen mountain so duplicated the smoke streaming from my chimney that I would wonder what campfire was lighted there and what wanderer sat beside it. When the moon appeared after nights of rain, I could not bear to be indoors. Everything must wait. The fire went out, and my supper chilled while I walked beside the rivers with the moon in my face. If I had not shared such moments with those among whom I dwelt, I would have felt myself an alien thing and not worthy of this high living.

Often it seemed that I lived between two worlds, for from the knoll in front of the cabin I could see Fireweed looming darkly above the Teal with mist concealing the fire-wracked slopes and clouds muffling the peaks; then I would turn directly around to find, between Cougar and Evergreen, a half-moon riding bright in a clear sky and the earth transmuted into a fairyland where no darkness could ever come. Even my clothesline became a thing of beauty, strung along its length with crystal moisture like a necklace of the moon. Sometimes the lamplight ran up almost to the top of the tall, straight trees of Home Wood, changing them into vast organ pipes with the rivers for their music.

To many my valley would seem a strange and lonely place, plunged down between dark mountains and shadowed by the darker forest. The sun never shines on its snow, except that of late February and March, and the great rains of spring and autumn shorten light and warmth still more. Winds come shrieking down through the passes, the rivers shout menacingly in flood and, during most of the year, two steel cables are my only connecting link with the outside world. Without them I would have two days' walk over the mountains before I could reach a settlement on my own side of the Teal. But what of all that? An hour's walk will bring the sun when, in December and January, the great longing for it comes. The cables and the tall trees to which they are attached will last, I hope, for my lifetime. I have no radio, no near neighbors— but I have more than these could ever give one.

> *Never any more to hurry, never to appear what I was not, never to be constrained by the crowd.*

Because there is "nothing too much" anywhere, life in my valley takes on zest and adventure as naturally as life in a city clothes itself in conformity and boredom. If I do not grow and prepare food, I starve; if I do not cut firewood, I freeze. It is as simple as that. There is always a feeling of being close to great events. If I become ill, I must cure myself—or die. If I am caught in a rockslide on one of my mountain rambles, if I fall into the swift, icy river of winter—then I shall see death come quickly. It is possible to meet a mountain lion on almost any trail, or even a grizzly who has drifted over from the eastern mountains. Fire lurks in the ever-present oil lamps and among the dry brush of summer and early fall. Any September I may see it tearing the heart out of a tall fir or devouring a stand of hemlock in gulping crunches.

Each day brings new problems and the need for keen wits with which to tackle them. I can never stand at my door on any morning and say: "I know how this day will be." I have lived in strange countries and in equally strange places of my own land, but not one of them has ever given me that sense of achievement and high adventure that I have found here. And "here" is so very small. The journeys I hope we shall take together in these pages will go only four miles west, two north, seven east, perhaps twelve south, eight thousand feet up and a spade's depth down. Such a little space to hold so much. But perhaps, "after we have made the just reckoning which retirement will help us to make, we shall begin to think the world in part measure mad and that we have been in a sort of bedlam all this time."

It is true that a little of this land is in my name and it is also true that I have used the words "my" and "mine" several times in referring to it—and shall probably do so on many more occasions. But they are not used in the ordinary interpretation of possession, for I have never felt that I "owned" anything here. It is mine only in the sense that it is part of me as I am of it. How foolish it would be to say I possessed something that can never be possessed, that has been here centuries before I came and will be here centuries after I am gone. I am only a transient tenant who wished to find, for a pinprick of eternity, succour and serenity; who wished to praise beauty and to share great living.

Whatever comes I shall have had this. I shall have known what it is to work with my hands and brain on my own land and for my own sustenance. I shall have known what it is to work for the community by labor traded back and forth and by supplying vegetables. I shall have known what it is to live completely alone with nature, for sometimes a whole winter will go by without a single human visitor. That is very good. It means that I can learn to know myself and to live with myself, that I can discover the ways of silence and beauty. There are long thoughts then and, I believe good ones, when

The soul selects her own society, Then shuts the door.

It is not the world that is shut out, but its clamour and impatience. Here, with my ear pressed close to the earth, I can listen to the very heart of humanity beating. From my primitive position I can evaluate civilization more truly and, freed from the pointless hurry and distraction of modern society, can appreciate for the first time the delicate nuances of living. The four freedoms are mine, but more than that I have a freedom of spirit that goes beyond and above them, a freedom that comes only when the soul has found itself.

I am not the same person who waded across the Teal that first August morning. I am the wind that comes down from the high hills; I am the deep forest, the singing rivers, the tall mountains. I am all of these things and more; I am the whole human being which they have made me.

Henceforth I ask not good fortune; I, myself am good fortune.
Henceforth I whimper no more, postpone no more, need nothing.

It is not even I who am writing these words now. I am only the means by which they are put down. The Spirit that is behind all the beauty of the world is the real author of this book. If there is failure in it, it is because the instrument is not yet clear and true enough.[8]

CHAPTER 5

Life in the Valley

Secure in her mountain haven, Douglas explored her surroundings and became acquainted with the denizens of the valley, both human and animal. As she came to know them, she felt an urgency about recording their lives. She realized they were part of a vanishing way of life—one which she hoped to commemorate and preserve through her writing. *River for My Sidewalk* contains many such portraits, for they "will soon be gone. I must write about it now so we shall not forget." This imperative is expressed in the first chapter of the book.

A WAY OF LIFE

A great deal is being written and said these days about "the Canadian way of life." But there is not just one method of Canadian living, there are a hundred or more. They share the heredity of freedom, but it is environment which shapes and changes them. They grow old and are pushed back into the chimney corner by a new generation of scientific discoveries or political ideas. They gradually dim in our memories and when we do think of them it is often with surprise that they could ever have existed. Many of us find it impossible to imagine any way of life which is different from the one we know now. Often we are too absorbed in the new to record the passing of the old.

Friends say to me: "Yes, there must be people who are interested in those wilderness stories of yours or they wouldn't sell so well, but why don't you write about things most of us know: cities, science, politics, sports?"

My answer is always the same: "Because you *do* know them. Because there are a thousand writers explaining those things, but only a handful to tell about my way of living. It will soon be gone. I must write about it now so we shall not forget."

Yes, it will soon be gone. The population of the earth is increasing and the wilderness is shrinking. As the necessity to produce becomes greater and our lives more and more regulated by government, it will be impossible for anyone to do as I have done: make an old miner's shack of 1860 into a comfortable home and live almost entirely off the country.

Everyone in the new world will have to produce something more practical than a few vegetables, some wilderness stories and a growth of soul. Probably most of the people who live then will find that crowded, ordered existence quite natural, for they will be products of the new age. But perhaps there will be some who will look up at the morning sky and wonder what it would be like to live always so close to nature that it is possible to hear the beating of earth's primeval heart.

I can tell them what it is like. It is the most wonderful thing that could ever happen to anyone. The hours in my Cascade mountain valley don't run by time clock or whistle; they are regulated much more grandly by the sun and moon. I get up at daylight and I go to bed at dark. If the moon happens to be bright before dawn arrives I get up then and steal a march on the day. I do own a clock, but I only look at it when I have to go "outside" or have promised to have a meal with one of my neighbours. Whether there is Daylight Saving or not makes no difference to me. It is not the regulated hour which is important, but the great simplicity of light.

The boss of my work is the weather. If it is fine then brush cutting, garden work, irrigation, expeditions for flower specimens, bird notes and photographs are the order of the day. If it rains then that is just the time to write, weed, hunt slugs or do the thousand and one workshop jobs which always seem to be ready and waiting for a rainy interlude. When snow covers the earth I shovel long paths to root house and river, saw and split my year's supply of wood, read and contemplate. All weather is good because there is always something good to be done. All time is good—but there is never enough of it for all the things I want to do. Yes, that I *want* to do. I cannot remember performing one task here that I did not thoroughly enjoy.

"Task – work"—they seem such strange words to apply to what I am doing. Anyone who knows what I accomplish here knows also that I work hard and long, yet all that I do is not work but delight. I even enjoy getting up in the morning. Who wouldn't if her alarm clock was the beautiful song of the hermit thrush, repeated over and over from a stump just outside the bedroom window? If the sun made a field of cloth of gold on high peaks and strode through the forest like an army with banners? If one could draw the precious air of freedom deep, deep into lungs and feel it quickening the heart until it wanted to shout for joy?

The day is my friend. I meet it with outstretched hand and use every moment of it to the utmost. Sitting in the house I have partially built I eat the food which I have grown for myself. I have tried to learn everything there is to know about the trees, flowers, birds, animals, insects and rocks which are all around me. It has taken me years and will take more years, but I feel that every grain of such knowledge brings me closer to the great harvest of the universe.

The night is my love. Dusk comes with the benediction of the thrush and the darkening of river water. The clearing is all shadow and the forest dim with mystery. The shade climbs higher and higher up the mountains which ring my valley, leaving only the peaks crested with sunlight. Everything becomes slower and more silent as the dusk deepens into night. Then stars burn silver in the sky and sometimes the moon sails a midnight sea to a port beyond the tall evergreens of Home Wood. This has been the way of night in the wilderness for untold eons. How few living now have ever known it as I do! Campers, fishermen, hunters come in here bringing their shouts and drinking and luxuries. They go home to boast of their wilderness adventures, but all they take away is a paste jewel in a plastic setting.

Little has changed here since this junction of the Teal and Wren rivers was first discovered by explorers thrusting out into unknown regions from the overland trails of the fur brigade. Coyotes still chase the mule deer, black bears still scoop ants from rotting logs, cougars still ambush the unwary grouse and scream through the mountain darkness. But there are few mink, otters or wolverines now, and the beaver is almost extinct. There are not many great trees left; only their stumps to remind us that giants once lived in this land. But the rivers still run singing from the hills with trout flashing in the greenstone-coloured water. Fir, hemlock and cedar—some of them two or three hundred years old—still crowd the forest, with willow, aspen and alder marching beside the streams. It is still possible to look in any direction and not see even a curl of smoke; to live the whole winter through—and most of the rest of the year—without sight or sound of a human being.

Many of us are or have been prospectors, placer or hard rock miners. That way of life is fast disappearing also. Soon there will be no one to recount the sagas of the gold hunters who trudged through searing deserts or ran white mountain water in dugout canoes. There will be no one to spice the histories of our present cities with roaring tales of their mining camp beginnings. The silver towns will fall into dust and there will be no one to revive them with legend and anecdote.

The modern prospector hunts the minerals of war and peace by plane and frequently comes back to civilization each night for his apple pie with ice cream. He has all the resources of this Age of Machines behind him. He can be reasonably sure that he will never spend his last days in a mountain cabin, packing dudes and panning gold each summer rather than take an old age pension—but happy as only that man can be who has a simple life, his own special brand of happiness and liberty bounded only by the rights of his neighbour.

All this is going—going. Let me tell of it now.

Douglas felt compelled to tell of the natural world, combining close observation and scientific study of the flora, fauna, and geography of her home ground with an appreciation of its aesthetic and spiritual value. Her holistic sense of the environment is succinctly phrased in the opening stanza of her poem "Life":

> This tree is part of life as I am part;
> These flowers, this weed, the little things that crawl
> Contain as I do, that unfailing heart
> Which is the sum and answer of us all.[1]

Her prolonged residence in one location afforded Douglas the opportunity to begin the intimate and recurring encounter with a beloved place that forms the basis for all nature writing. She knew that her writing opened her to the charge of being a sentimentalist but felt her topic too profoundly to be put off by this.

Oh, yes, I know all the modern tabus on "sentimental nature writing," on assuming that animals can talk in their own way and that plants react to people. Maybe it is all silly sentiment. I don't know. But I do know that persons react to places, just as they do to other people. According to their sensitivity, they react sharply or sluggishly to what in a human being would be called personality. Certainly it has always been that way with me. I have been in places I liked at first glimpse, places I distrusted, places I wanted to leave as quickly as possible. Always in the back of my mind was the desire for that one perfect place where I could feel fulfilled and truly at home.[2]

In return for her dedication to observing and preserving the world around her, Douglas achieved a sense of well-being and satisfaction.

Now there is a hiatus in time: winter is nearly over, spring has not quite begun. I feel suspended in time, as though I belonged to nothing and were going nowhere. It is a good feeling. Although my physical radius is more and more restricted as the rains pour down and the trails become slippery with ice, yet my spiritual radius grows larger and larger until at last I realize that I belong to the whole universe and not just to one little planet in it.

I believe very strongly that it would be an excellent thing for the world if everyone could be isolated in this way for some period of their lives. . . .[3]

*"View from my
living-room door."*

*"The forest
at my back door."*

"The Wren in summer."

In the vegetable garden the greens are growing.

*Nature's garden
is beautiful also.*

"Fire sweeping across Cougar Mountain."

*"The next morning
shows a haze of smoke
over Evergreen."*

*"Tumbled mountains
and lightning-slashed tree
make the canyon scenery
wild and beautiful."*

"Delta of the Coquihalla, but here the seemingly quiet waters are trying to push the Fraser over against the mountain."

"Starvation Creek, which runs into the Teal outside my door."

"Frost fires melting in the sun."

"Mountain sunset."

"Nothing like a full woodshed for warm feet and a quiet mind."

But Douglas was not always alone. She had frequent visitors who had to brave forest trails and ford rivers to get to her—but get there they did. Her directions are inscribed in her poem "Bush Map":

> It is as easy to walk here
> as it is to follow
> a city street.
> Keep the sound of the river clear
> on your right, to the hollow
> where twin-flower, neat
> as your garden bed, runs over
> old cedar logs and bent
> vine maples brush
> the bleeding-heart and the clover.
> Turn as the river went
> last spring; through lush
> and blue-eyed grasses—quite dry now—
> then bear hard to your left
> for half a mile
> to the woods where a hemlock bough
> lying within a cleft
> of rock by a pile
> of stones marks the trail's beginning.
> Now you can't miss the way;
> it is clearly
> blazed right to the sudden thinning
> of spruce and fir where gay
> hyssop nearly
> crowds in on my little garden.
> Come on up tomorrow.
> I hope you see
> my hermit thrush, he's a—pardon?
> You may want to borrow
> a map from me?
> But it's as easy to walk here
> as it is to follow
> a city street.
> Keep the sound of the river clear—[4]

She also recounted the travails of her visitors in "Visiting the Hard Way," a chapter from *River for My Sidewalk*. After following the trail, often in "Stygian" darkness, the visitor reached the ultimate test—crossing the river on a tiny platform that swung across on a fragile cable.

I have often wished that I could read the minds of some of my guests when they arrive at the source of this wild music and see the spray of that swift mountain river, the Teal, flashing white against the blackness of night and deep water. Surely some of the awe an explorer feels when coming upon an unknown wilderness stream must touch them then. But when they realize that they must climb a sixteen-foot home-made ladder to a frail platform part way up a giant fir and suspended over this raging torrent, their expressions show distinctly modified delight. The platform has no railing, so you can step off into space quite easily—but there is really no good reason to do so. The cage—two wide boards fastened by wires to roller bearings running on a thick wire rope—swings there, held to the tree by a looped wire and hook. It will accommodate two passengers with packs or three without luggage, and it tips easily around the edges. I've lost a trout and a chocolate cake that way, but never a guest.

The first passengers get on board and grip the cable above them with both hands to keep the cage from starting ahead of schedule after it is unhooked and before the last passenger can leap aboard. Then away we go, sliding easily and swiftly along the cable through the darkness with one small lantern swinging at our prow. It is quite a thrill for those who think all transportation began with the motor car. But from this side— where the platform is considerably higher than the home landing—it is a quick, easy ride through the night. The pull uphill coming back will take longer and be harder work. This arrangement works well, however, as the biggest loads come in and anyone who goes "outside" is usually travelling light.

Soon we are climbing the stone steps to my clearing and going down the path to where my cabin makes a deeper shadow against the darkness of forest and mountain. In summer daylight, with the birds singing matins and the garden in full summer bloom, my guests exclaim with amazement and delight. But when we arrive in this gloom and, except for the rivers, silence; when they can sense the wildness and solitude all around them, then they are very quiet—wondering, possibly, why on earth they ever accepted my invitation.

While Gilean welcomed guests, she had strict rules for their visits.

GUESTS
A WORD IN TIME SAVES HOARSNESS

1… Please park all unkindness, gossip, intolerance, impatience, anger, and worry on the cage platform across the Coquihalla. There is no room for it here.

2… A tool in the hand is worth six in the bush—so please put that hammer back when you've finished with it.

3… Broiled chops are delicious, but broiled guests are a pain in more than the neck. Please ask for the suntan oil before cooking begins.

4… Share the work to share the play—and K.P. duty is of both the male and female gender!

5… Hermit thrush lullabies supplied at dusk and robin alarm clocks at dawn. We recommend these hours for tangled nerves. Also coal oil is scarce.

6… Poets, musicians, artists—here are mountains, forests and rivers for your delight! Make the most of them and you will make me happy.

Otherwise, there are no strings attached to this visit. You may walk your shoes through or sleep the day away; talk your head off or imitate the clam; eat your meals up on the roof or down in the irrigation ditch. I am so glad to have you here and I shall be so sorry to see you go.

COME AGAIN—AND STAY LONGER![5]

Now entering middle age, Gilean Douglas's certainty about the rights of women and her acknowledgement of her own need for independence were becoming more sure. She continued to write articles about gender inequities and the problems of marriage. Still, there were many men in her life. One of her main admirers was Philip Major, a married army officer stationed in Vancouver, who was later to play an important role in Douglas's life.

But in Home Wood, alone or with visitors, she celebrated the seasons as they turned and the simple pleasures of her rural life. Always a great fan of Christmas, Douglas wrote about the unexpected pleasures of spending the holiday "alone."

MERRY CHRISTMAS TO ALL

All day the snow had been coming down; big white flakes that seemed to be falling of their own weight, though they were really as light as the thistledown they covered in my clearing. All day the music of the rivers had been fading, until now it was only a thread of sound—or was it memory? All day the high mountains surrounding my valley had been softly receding. Then they disappeared entirely and opal filled the air where they had been.

It was evening and in the mellow light from my living-room oil lamp the six-sided space ships came softly, unhurriedly to earth in their tens of trillions. The paths to the rivers, shovelled that morning, were buried again in crystals and beyond them the uncleared trails had become one with drift and rise and hollow. On the fire-scarred mountain I must climb to reach the nearest house four miles away, the snow would be waist deep by now. Too deep for me, loaded with a packsack of gifts and city clothes. This was not ski country and my bearpaw snowshoes had been loaned and lost.

Two days before Christmas and my plans in tatters? Plans to get up at 3 a.m. and walk over the mountain to connect with a speeder leaving at six for the nearest railroad station. (The branch line had been closed down since the first snowfall in October.) There I was to catch a train for city celebrations in the home of friends. Now I would do none of this at all but spend Christmas, New Year's and probably the rest of the winter snowed in with solitude.

For a few moments I thought regretfully of baths and lights and of warmth which I didn't have to axe into existence; of that glorious promised turkey and the sparkling shop windows. Most of all I thought of good talk and good friends. The door to all this had been slammed shut in my face and as I unpacked the rucksack I would have carried to town I took out a few bright expectations too. But I have always believed that when one door closes another opens. So a door had opened now for me. Where was it and what was behind it?

Having forgotten to reset the time clock in my mind, I woke up promptly at 3 a.m. The cabin, flake insulated, was hardly cold though the temperature must have been in its teens. Snowlight and fading moonlight—(the moon had gone down behind the mountains)—gave my bedroom a Regal lily shining. White, blue and pale cerise frost flowers bloomed on every windowpane in this translucency and I grew some of my own by holding a lighted match to "beds" of granular frost. Ferns, fronds and feathers were everywhere, with many Christmassy garlands; and how delighted I was to find the Tannenbaum, the fir tree, over and over again.

But now there was my own Christmas tree to discover, wood to carry, paths to shovel, evergreens to cut for decoration, river ice to break for water, more treats to find for the animals and birds I hoped would come to share them. I went spinning like a top from one inside job to another and then burst out the door into a world of wonder. So still, so white, so gloriously shining; so tall and vast, so utterly filled with snow and solitude. And I, this little I, in the middle of it all. O Life, O Life, I kept saying, this is too much. You have made it all too beautiful. I can hardly bear it.

The snow still fell, but lightly now and I noticed that the flakes were smaller and simpler than the complex forms of yesterday. They had come from the highest clouds, the cirro and the cirrostratus, where lunar and solar halos originate. In fact, the halos are made by light passing through the ice crystals uninterruptedly, from one hexagonal face to another. Light, light, it seemed to run through me like a current that wakened to ecstasy every nerve and vein and sinew. I hugged myself with joy.

The snow stopped, but I didn't. I strung rose hips and western dogwood berries, popcorn I had grown and red huckleberries I had put down in jars. All for the young fir at the forest's edge which would be my living, growing Christmas tree.

Green cookies would go on it and golden doughnuts, scarlet apples, carrot candles, turnip and beet balls. I would share it with the birds, though already their own tree was decorated with suet, seeds in fat, seeds in honey and sunflower seeds alone for the jays and varied thrushes. There was always food on the feeding tray, but this was special.

No browse for the deer, for they were yarded up miles away and the snow between was deep. Porridge with sweet fruit in it for the old coyote, and stew for the wildcat who both came around for a handout, now and then. In case the old and almost toothless cougar arrived he would have both, a washbowl of it near the Christmas tree. The bears would be hibernating surely and the birds wouldn't start coming until dawn. Except for the owls, of course.

Just before dusk I went inside to stir up the fire, but I put on no lights. Munching a sandwich I sat down by the window to watch. The sky had cleared and behind Cougar Mountain the moon was rising. The snow sparkled wherever light touched it and the world outside was a child's dream story before life crumpled the page. But as the moon rose my hopes fell, for two hours had gone by and no guests had come to the feast. Would they come? Would there be a stranger among them to invoke the old Celtic blessing? "Often, often, often goes the Christ in the Stranger's guise."

Then a grey shadow stirred as the coyote sidled slowly out of the cabin's darker shade. He went to the big bowl of porridge placed on the kitchen side of the house, where he usually fed. At that moment I realized that the wildcat bowl was in use too—and was that a lean tawny movement near the forest woodpile? Were those the golden eyes of a great grey owl in the hemlock?

But I forgot them all when I spotted a furry form rolling up the path from the river. A bear, looking like a two-year-old. No, not the same one which had been romping up and down the river all summer, gorging himself on berries. That one had a sharper face. This one hardly seemed to notice his fellow diners, but headed straight for the bird tree—and honey.

I tore into the kitchen, opened a jar of fish and tossed this towards him. The coyote and wildcat jumped away, but came cautiously back again. While bruin was trying to get fish out of the snow I opened more jars. As he was on the seventh, the forest woodpile seemed to lengthen and the old cougar came out into the moonlight. In its kind glow he appeared almost young and invincible. The bear raised his head and looked at him. Then he grabbed up the last piece of fish and ambled rather hastily down the garden path. When I looked around my holiday table was empty, except for the ancient one enjoying his porridge-stew and I taking another sandwich out of my pocket.

But for a short while we had all been there, in peace and acceptance; cougar, coyote, wildcat, bear, owl and human. For those moments there had been something between us. A truce? No, more than that; a bond. I became truly part of all life then and for a flash I saw how earth might have been. I was not even startled; only surprised that they had not spoken and the old tales of animals talking on Christmas Eve come alive—again? But perhaps we did "talk" together. The stars glittered, the moon silver-coated the snow, the cougar and I ate. I felt that the others were not too far away, watching.

At least one of them came back, for next morning both trees were wrecks and it didn't look like owl work. But it didn't matter either. I fixed them up again before the birds arrived and Christmas Day feasting began.

That day was a dream of heaven, blue and white and shining. I went through it on wings and wings were all around me; chickadee, wren, kinglet, jay, kingfisher, blackbird, varied thrush, creeper, nuthatch, grosbeak, bunting, redstart, water ouszel and even a willow ptarmigan down from the peaks.

After dark, a pygmy owl hushed in, a saw-whet owl perched on my ridgepole and later still a horned owl came looking for mice that were looking for crumbs. Three of my four-footed friends returned, though not the bear. But he had played the Stranger's part and I was blessed indeed. Now I knew what door had opened and that it would never open for me again in just this way. I looked up at the mountains and the sapphire sky to say thank you, thank you. It seemed so pitifully little for all I had been given.[6]

Her years in the Cascade Mountains were pivotal for Gilean Douglas. Working the land and celebrating the world around her through her writing offered a way into a new state of being. Here she found both home and a beloved in a place—a corner of the wilderness that became intimately familiar. Like many nature writers, she pursued the paradox that in losing one's self in nature, in losing a sense of personal neediness, she came to a more profound sense of identity.

CHAPTER 6

Paradise Lost

The cycle of the seasons continued. While Douglas frequently travelled outside her mountain fastness, her emotional centre remained there. There, too, she suffered no lack of inspiration, and she wrote prolifically in the 1940s. In addition to her two prose works and many poems, she wrote journalistic articles and compiled material for planned books on the plants and birds of the area around her cabin. She was particularly pleased to note that she was amassing a very long list of bird life for a place said to be deficient in birds. She also kept a mountain journal upon which she hoped to base further articles and books.

Though physically rigorous, and to most outsiders austere, Douglas's life was rich in simple pleasures—especially once the summer sun allowed "Roman bathing" to begin.

The best size for a bathroom is as big as all outdoors. Sky-blue ceiling, evergreen walls, sanded brown floor and superbly air-conditioned—the bathroom I have betters all the plans of all the architects for the streamlined houses of an atomic world. If I wish, I can use a new tub each morning, and there are no heating restrictions. Lying in one of the many pools left between the boulders by the receding river with hot stones underneath me and the water a foot deep, I can fairly simmer. For a bracing rinse afterward there are the cool, green depths of that big pool, Dubh Glas.

Two hours of weeding and spraying make an excellent appetizer for a bath, especially when heightened by the thought that "there is no ancient gentlemen but gardeners . . . they hold up Adam's profession." The sun is just above the mountains then and the cabin, when I go back to it for soap and towel, is dark and cool. Robin, warbler and thrush are making morning music while a calliope hummingbird is vibrating over a patch of sunlit clarkia. Bee flies and butterflies are warming themselves, and an ant lion, belying his name, goes delicately by. Halfway down the path to the Teal a shaft of sunlight strikes across late-blooming blue and yellow iris and the budding sweet william beside them. It lights up the many small beds and rock gardens in this part of the grounds and floods the stumps that brim with pansy, alyssum and dwarf wallflower.

The vegetable gardens and strawberry beds—"Doubtless God could have made a better berry, but doubtless God never did"—are in full sun and so is the large flowerbed on the knoll where jasmine, heuchera, phlox and matricaria live amicably together. Then past the dewy gold and flame of Mrs. Dupont and Paul Scarlet, the colorful disorder of the wildflower bed and down the stone steps that divide the big rock garden fronting the Teal. To the left, on the flat below, beans, peas, potatoes and sugar beets show blossom, leaf and pod. To the right, on a small island that has the Wren on one side and a dry—except in early spring and late fall—watercourse on the other, my water tank and tower stand almost hidden among the trees. Chamomile—which I like to call mayweed—spreads a white carpet at the base, with woolly sunflower and purple fleabane weaving through it, like Assyrian cohorts in purple and gold. . . .

A bath tub—quickly! Here is a splendid one, almost encircled by boulders. The water is over a foot deep and warmer than the Gulf of Mexico. The stones at the bottom are smooth and rounded and I can lie full-length with ease. Ah, this is heaven! I prop my head on a rock and stretch out, covered with water to my chin, looking up into the clear face of the summer sky. A dipper goes into his song and dance on a rock nearby, and a kingfisher, from his gallery seat on the cage cable, gives a Bronx cheer. A mourning cloak butterfly alights beside me, dark against the dazzling white of limestone, and makes rhythm with its wings. The sun strikes full on rocks and river and the reflection hurts my eyes. I close them and relax in the warmth of the water. . . .[1]

The warm months were heavenly, but winter had its own special appeal. Douglas lovingly described the delights of that season as well.

Slowly, slowly the evergreen of the mountains has retreated before the steady advance of snow. Then one evening I look out the window and the soft languid flakes are falling in the lamplight. They fall all night, while the voice of the river becomes more and more hushed and the noises of the forest die away. By dawn the whole world of stream and wood and mountain has been kindled to a white flame of beauty.

There is nothing quite like the first snow. I go out in the early morning and there is such silence that even breath is a profanation. The mountain to the north has a steel-blue light on it and to the west the sky still holds something of the darkness of night. To the east and south a faint, very faint, pink is beginning to spread. I look up and see the morning star keeping white watch over a white world.

Soon the whole sky is azure and flamingo, but still the silence holds. Every branch of every tree is weighted with cold and stillness; every stump is crowned with crystal; every fallen log is overlaid with silver. The wild berry bushes have puffballs of jeweler's cotton here and there along their branches and even the stark roots of hemlocks and cedars have become grottos of quartz and chrysolite. And the silence holds.

The sky is clear blue now and the sun has flung diamonds down on meadow and bank and wood. Beauty, the virgin, walks here quietly, quietly. She is telling her pearls, and her feet make no sound and no sign upon the immaculate snow. The silence is dense and deep; it is like nothing else.

Then the night comes, and the silence holds. The moon is high with a dark-blue sky behind it and with mountains, plains and forests of silver lying below. The trees, the bushes and the tall ferns are carved with alabaster; the meadows and lawns are white satin set with diamonds. The earth is whole; it is immutable. In this candid perfection the heart is hushed and even thought seems blasphemy. What mind can hold this beauty? What words can define it? Still the silence holds.

There is a feeling about this season that is in no other. It is a sense of snugness, security and solitude; its "beauty is eternity gazing at itself in a mirror." There will be no human visitors now until spring and nothing to disturb long hours of work and contemplation. Only the bark walls and the windows of the little cabin show between the white-laden roof and the white drifts around, yet the whole building seems to be more solid, more firmly rooted. At night golden lamplights stream out over the snow, and smoke from the fireplace rises straight up into the clear, still air. Such a picture of warmth and contentment! It is hard to know which is better—to be outside looking in at such a scene, or to be inside looking out at the sparkling stars, the bright mountains shouldering a night-blue sky and all the calm clarity of wintered earth.

Sometimes when we are alone we are in the best company. By "alone" I mean away from people, for actually we are never completely by ourselves. Can I say that I am solitary when I may discuss friendship with Emerson, war and peace with Tolstoy, nature with Thoreau, and history with Carlyle, Gibbon and a dozen others? Where, in any city or countryside, could I ever hope to find such great minds and gather them around my fireside?[2]

Throughout each year, Douglas found life stimulating and delightful. She continued corresponding with her wide circle of friends and was planning for a visit from an old friend, Fran Dietrich, when disaster struck.

Tuesday, May 6th, 1947

Fran

I am writing this sitting beside the ashes of my home—the realest home that I have had since I was a child.

The ashes are still smoking and so hot that I cannot look much for even the one or two things which might be left. The fire began last night at 8.30 and by 8.40 the ceiling of the living-room had fallen and the whole house was just flames. It was less than five minutes before the sparks and brands were flying down from the ceiling as I made the only three trips I could to rescue things. I could only run with them a few yards from the house and on the last trip my pajamas—I had just gone to bed—were smoking and I could smell my hair burning as brands fell on my head. I have quite a bad burn just at the top and my eyes are all cloudy—scorched, I suppose—so that I can hardly see. Even the clothes which I managed to save—a very few—are most of them scorched. The movie camera with the film for you has gone, my watch (the good aviator one), what jewelry I had there, all my linen and all the food I had laid in for the whole summer. I had bought coffee and cereals for you and there was just everything there that we could want. I have never known a place which had so many little comforts and something of everything for they were things I had bought over nine years and things I had built in myself down there since last year. Over 200 books—all gone except seven. I saved the flower and Audubon book, but Taverner's birds went and all my reference books and the good ones—not a novel among them that I had saved for so many years. They were my friends.

I had just finished painting the house inside and out and it was shining. I had upholstered two chairs with lovely material I had been saving for years. Inside it was celestial red and Dutch blue and there was one window corner which was so lovely. There were a table and chair there of blue and on the window sill two vases made for bookends which I had filled with daffodils. I took a picture of them. How I hope it will turn out. I had taken several pictures that day—and I have taken others this morning. The last ones.

Outside the beds were a mass of daffodils, yellow wild violets, heuchera, pansies, English daisies, wild bleeding-heart, twisted stalk, miner's lettuce, hyacinths and the tulips were just beginning to bloom. All the vegetables were coming up so greenly and I had that very last day taken the very last weed from the whole garden. It was perfect and so was the house inside. I was even caught up on every last bit of sewing. Everything was shining. The little house was so beautiful. You know, Fran, it was the loveliest little house I have ever seen, although it was so simple—or perhaps because of that—and so woodsy. If the little house had to die she died when she was most beautiful and there was a song sparrow to sing her requiem over her pyre at dawn. It was the way she would have liked to go. I am glad for that. But I loved her so. All my work and my heart had gone into her. It was the one place in the world I could call my own—and the place so beautiful!

"A February thaw has coated the trees with ice."

"White silence closed down on forest and clearing."

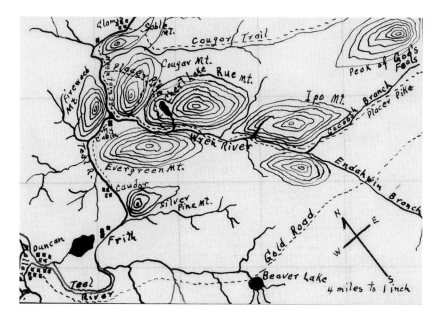

Map of paradise.

*"I follow the river into
the mountains and sleep out
a winter night."*

Snow and sun
weave a
winter tapestry.

*"Now my Eden was just as I had visualized it,
even to the teal-blue doors and windows of the cabin."*

*"If the little house had to die she died when she was most beautiful,
and there was a song-sparrow to sing her requiem over her pyre at dawn."*

I do not know what I am going to do now. I am staying with neighbors until Saturday and then going into V. I have wired Phil and heard from him. He will come here Saturday night to look after posting signs and locking the roothouse with the things which were in the woodshed. Prospectors and others are wandering all over the country now—there are two down there this morning—and when a place has burned so many people think it has been abandoned also. I would go back there and live in a tent tomorrow and try to build again—if only I were healthy and strong. But how could I ever carry in all the things that would have to go there now and I can't impose on my neighbors any more. My heart is acting badly now and I can't stop crying yet. I will soon, but now surely there can be tears for so much beauty and delight. I was so happy there, so terribly happy. The one place where I could sleep and work and where I could go when everything and everyone else failed. But it isn't just that: it is the little house itself with all its spirit of love, its personality, its feeling of friendliness. The doors were blue, Fran—like the window-boxes —and they opened so wide.

I just don't know, Fran. I shall have to write you again as soon as I get in the city. I shall talk things over with Phil on Saturday. Please send me any ideas you have. All I know is that I must plant again and work and sleep again and work in the quiet sun and the fresh wind. But I must plant somewhere something that I shall reap.

My love goes to you and my great sorrow that you will never see my home now and know its peace and loveliness.[3]

The paradise Gilean Douglas had been slowly building through her labour and writing was destroyed. The loss of her beloved mountain home stayed with Douglas until the end of her life as yet another experience of expulsion from a safe haven. In another letter written right after the fire, to her friend Louise Meginness, she expresses the event in Biblical terms: "I had so little time. The moccasins were smoking on my feet, a brand fell on top of my head and gave me a very bad burn, sparks fell on the clothes I was carrying . . . and there was no time, no time."[4]

In "Lost Eden," written five years after the devastating fire, she expresses her continued longing and love for that "home of the heart" where she had spent the seven happiest years of her life.

I have learned in the last five years that it is not wise to look too closely or too long at those high peaks [of the Coast Mountains], especially if an olive-backed thrush is singing good-night. Neither is it wise to walk through the woods of early morning when a song sparrow is hymning the sun. Better, far better, to talk, to smile, to shorten the zestful stride to steps as decorous as any mourner's. For who has ever gone back to Eden? . . .

That morning [the day of the fire] I did my last spring work on the flower beds and put the last touch of paint on house and outbuildings. I worked even harder than usual and hardly paused for lunch. Somehow I wanted to get everything finished that day, although I could think of no good reason why I should. But before five it was all completed. When I walked around on a final tour in inspection I realized that this was the first time in seven years that there hadn't been a job of physical work clamoring to be done. Now my Eden was just as I had visualized it, even to the teal-blue doors and windows of the cabin. The woodshed was filled, heater wood piled high outside, the roothouse whitewashed so as to show off the many full jars better and in the workshop each tool had its place. I got my camera out and began taking pictures from both sides of the river.

But instead of feeling satisfied I was restless and when a neighbor shouted from across the Rinn I was glad to go over and collect the boxes of food and oddments which he had so kindly packed in for me. He was going farther along and couldn't stay for supper. I started to get my own, unwrapping parcels and putting things away in between times. At dusk when I went into the bedroom to get ready for bed, I thought that the house was hotter than I had ever known it at this time of year.

It was just as I got into pajamas and dressing-gown that I heard the explosion, like a big gun going off right over my head. What in the world? As I stood there wondering I heard a crackling noise as though there was a fire in the heater. But there wasn't. Rushing out into the living-room I saw flames licking through the ceiling just over my desk and one look was enough to tell me that the cabin was doomed. Later I was to discover that the bang had been a spontaneous dust explosion in the attic, which had been built without louvers; the same sort of thing that happens sometimes with hay in a barn when there has been a long spell of wet weather followed by intense heat.

I grabbed for manuscripts, filing cards, typewriter—everything I could carry that had to do with my work as a writer. When my arms were full I dashed outside and flung the things down on the ground away from the cabin. Then I rushed inside again and began pulling precious books from the shelves. I saved only seven of the most valuable—which happened to be also the largest—out of more than 200 that I had collected for reference over many years and most of which could never be replaced. But the ceiling was blazing and there was so little time—so little time. As I stood by one of the bookcases I looked up and saw yellow daffodils standing on a window-sill in a blue-green vase. Wildly I thought: "I must take that window with me!" Strange what ideas come to one at such moments.

On my third trip I threw open the cupboard doors and grabbed up shoes and clothes, more books—anything I could lay my hands on. As I ran across the living-room with them sparks fell in showers from the burning ceiling and clothes, dressing-gown and even my hair began to smoulder. When I threw down my load and turned to go back a fourth time, the ceiling fell in with a crash and the little cabin became an inferno of flames. By the watch I had saved it had been just seven minutes since the fire started. So short a time in which to lose almost all I had in the world.

Stumps began to blaze here and there in the clearing from the great heat of the blazing cedar walls. A curl of smoke went up from some of the papers I had dropped too near the cabin and when I went to rescue them and my typewriter I had to crawl along the ground shielding my face with one arm. I scorched my fingers on the handle of the metal typewriter case as I pulled it to safety.

There was hardly any wind, but I realized that if the woodshed and particularly the forest were to be saved that I must do it. Outside the kitchen door, where the wall had not begun to burn, I found two buckets and filled them at the river. Then began my night-long work of salvation. Beyond the range of that unholy light of fire there was only darkness and solitude. I didn't hear the little wind in the evergreens, the shouting of the river; there was nothing left in the world for me except buckets to be filled and emptied and filled again. I stamped out sparks, I beat out small blazes with my hands, I took off my dressing-gown and used it to smother a leaping rush of flame. At one period I remember thinking: "My heart won't take much more of this. It will have to be the forest or me." But of course I chose the forest—and when dawn came I was still alive too.

I stood on what remained of my lawn and looked about me. The flames had died down, but the great mass of ashes which had been my home was still too hot to handle. Glass and metal had fused together, tin had exploded and now lay in blackened heaps. The great sill beams were charred and shrunk to half their size. Here and there a tool with all its temper gone thrust up from the ruins. But the woodshed and roothouse were untouched and only those flowers had died which were in the beds immediately around the house.

Everywhere else daffodils blew golden in the wind, echoed by the wild yellow violet, hyacinth, crocus, Lenten rose, grape hyacinth, bluebell, lily-of-the-valley, pansy, quaint English daisy, tulip bud and wild pink currant that filled my valley with color and beauty. Beyond them lay the vegetable plots with their long green rows and beyond that the singing river. Little rosy clouds floated across a deep blue sky above green mountains, as they had done in so many spring dawns. But except for the Rinn's voice there was a hush more tangible than any I had ever known, even at the hushed break of day.

Suddenly it was broken by a silver lilt of notes from a thimbleberry bush only a few yards away from me. Again and again came the rush of trills, the song sparrow's lovely song. As I listened to it something that had been very heavy and silent on my heart seemed to lighten and dissolve. I threw myself down on what remained of the green grass and I am not ashamed to say that I lay there and cried for all the beautiful years that were only ashes now.

Not only the years, but the work that had gone into them. Many manuscripts had burned, including a 125,000 word book on wildflowers of the Selkirks which I had illustrated with my own photographs. Nearly 100,000 words of another book and only a little less than that of a third had gone, together with many files, negatives and all my flower collection. My library too, of course, and all the many other things that I had gathered round me so slowly and so happily.

But if my little cabin had to die I was glad it could go when it was most beautiful: painted and polished and shining with my heart's love. Even the last weed pulled from the garden and the last bit of furniture made. I was glad, too, that there was a song sparrow to sing its requiem over the pyre at dawn—and that in my mind's sight nothing could change now. Firelight would still shine on my rows of books, the cedar-panelled walls would gleam like satin, the deep red rugs would glow on the dark floors with the Dutch blue furniture standing on them invitingly. The green roof would always speak softly to the tile-red porches, the teal-blue window-boxes spill over with flowers and the teal-blue doors stand wide open to life and beauty.

But late that afternoon—after I had thrown the blown and blackened cans into the river, laid the charred beams neatly and raked earth over ashes—I crossed the Rinn on the way to my neighbors. When I reached the other side I looked back from the platform, where I had stood so often looking down at bark walls, shake roof and smoking chimney. Now, if I had been a stranger, I would never have known that any home had stood there at all. I couldn't see the woodshed and roothouse. Everywhere else there was only greenness growing in the spring wind with spring flowers starring it. It was at that moment I thought my heart would really break.[5]

CHAPTER 7

Arrival: Cortes

*A*fter the fire, alone and again a wanderer, Gilean Douglas was taken in by friends on Keats Island, near Gibsons (northwest of Vancouver, British Columbia). With literally no roof over her head and very few clothes on her back, she began to try to put her world back together. Most urgent was her need to find another home. Her first secure haven since the death of her father was gone, and its loss was a devastation to the spirit she never forgot. Her sense of exile is expressed in a poem written shortly after she left her valley for the last time.

OLD PROSPECTOR

The small waves run, in this complaisant land,
tinkling and trite along a sheltered shore
and everything is ready to the hand
with no rich need for struggle any more.

And here, they told me, I could be secure
and here, they said, I would find ease and rest
with day a windless voyage, mapped and sure,
and night a harbour undisturbed and blessed.

What's that to me—I who have lived alone
where mountains are a shout against the sky
and gnawed upon a lean, toil-sweetened bone
wrested from earth and rock to primal cry.

> I who have faced the wind from alpine snow
> and walked by star and heard the hill stream's song
> of waterfall and canyon; I who know
> the friendship of the swift and dark and strong.
>
> Hold out to me no word of gentleness
> in sun upon flat sand, of days to fill
> with neighbour chat. I shall take nothing less
> than fight and storm and silence when I will.[1]

Part of the process of rebuilding her life involved coming to terms with her relationship with Philip Major, whom she had met in 1945. Phil was married and had two teenaged children, but he had visited Gilean occasionally at her cabin. They had also been corresponding steadily, even daily, and the relationship had progressed to the point where they signed themselves "your husband" and "your wife." Phil began to negotiate a divorce and to try to arrange matters so that they could be together. Gilean was more hesitant, wary of a new relationship after the failures of the past. Yet, as she had in the past, she once more turned to a man's courting as a solution to the ache of homelessness.

Characteristically, the relationship lived in and through correspondence transcended the face-to-face encounter. In their daily letters, Gilean and Phil were at peace. For Gilean, the romance in writing was far more satisfactory than the reality of being together, but Phil continued to press for marriage. Gilean had continued to affirm the possibility of a wedding while delaying its occurrence, but the loss of her home in May of 1947 changed the situation considerably.

Until the spring of 1948, the two debated the merits of returning to the mountains. They also debated whether or not to marry. In a letter to Phil the spring after the fire, Gilean expressed her "tremendous feeling of despair":

> If I had this feeling before a trip or anything else I would immediately cancel whatever I was going to do. It does seem ironical that in something much more important than any trip I am trying to ignore the feeling entirely. I am trying to be absolutely honest and to tell you what I have figured out may lie behind it. Here are the reasons as I see them: my previous unhappiness in marriage, my almost certainty that you will not *continue* to be happy under such conditions as I shall need (no matter how much you think so now), loss of freedom and

independence, interference and possible arrival of Marjorie and/or the children, realization of my need for change of scene and climate which I can't possibly have again because of finances . . . and my present health. . . . Please don't just be angry and say that everything is over. Please try to help me. Surely there is some more light that can be thrown on this. You are my friend as well as my love. You are the only family I have to go to in my trouble."[2]

The conflict between her needs and her fears seemed resolved when Phil found an island property that satisfied their mutual desire for an acreage that could be used as a farm. Later, in *The Protected Place*, Douglas summarized the criteria they had set:

When I advertised for a home—not realizing that I would get even more than that—I put in everything I wanted. I asked for a stream, timber, old orchard, barn, habitable house, separate cottage, waterfront, view, seclusion.

"Well, of course, all you want is heaven," said the girl in the newspaper office who read my ad.

"No," said another girl, reading over her shoulder. "She hasn't asked for golden streets. It sounds more like fairyland to me."[3]

Rescuing the abandoned Poole homestead on Cortes Island—137 acres with a small house and outbuildings—seemed more feasible than trying to rebuild in the mountains, with all its difficulties of access. Gilean bought the island property on "Channel Rock" sight unseen in 1948, and Phil moved up that summer to begin the work of reclaiming the old homestead. She remained based on Keats Island but travelled to eastern Canada for a speaking tour, and to California and Nevada to visit friends, gather writing material, and seek the sun.

Apparently the way was cleared for the marriage and the move to Cortes, yet Gilean continued to express misgivings. In a letter written in February 1948, she still held out the possibility of returning to the mountains, but to "a place which is more accessible." While she realized that Cortes was more practical, she worried, "How can I live away from my mountains and my rivers forever? The longing for them is a great ache in me all the time."[4] Gilean's reluctance to sever her connection to the mountains was revealed by her continued possession of the property there, which she owned until the end of her life. Her ambivalence about marriage also persisted.

While protesting love, she was unsettled by Phil's inability to ready the Cortes property for her arrival.

> We had planned our whole life on the premise that you would finish the cottage and get everything ready so that I would have a comfortable and quiet place in which to work and earn our living. You have been there eight months and the place is still, except for the garden and outside things, much as when you went up there. It is no reluctance on my part to face hard living—I have had a lot of that—but it is a distinct reluctance to go once again into a place where I shall have to supply the drive and much of the work to make it into a home, at the same time struggling to get my own work done.[5]

In the end, Gilean agreed to marry Phil, but only under strict conditions. Since he had no financial resources to bring to the marriage and would have no source of income until the farm began to produce, she undertook to provide the financing, including Phil's monthly support payments to his former wife, through her writing and from the remnants of her inheritance. In return, he was to do everything else: building, gardening, meals, and housekeeping. Further, she demanded a prenuptial agreement in which Major agreed to make his will in her favour, while granting her the right to dispose of her property as she saw fit. Since he had children, this concession was remarkable, as was his agreement to take Douglas's name.

The marriage took place in Vancouver on June 1, 1949, and Gilean finally joined Phil on Cortes. Whaletown, when the newlyweds arrived, was a tiny settlement on an island tucked in among other islands about one hundred miles upcoast from Vancouver. Its name was misleading because, as Douglas wrote, Whaletown "has no whales and is no town. It is a community of about thirty families scattered hither and yon over the northwest part of an attractive island that's twenty by seven miles in area."[6]

At that time, access to Cortes Island was difficult. Provincial ferry service did not exist until 1970, and the tiny settlement had to care for itself and provide all necessities for the body and the spirit. Channel Rock, which to this day can be reached only by a two-mile hike over a rough trail or by a two-mile boat trip from Whaletown, was isolated even by island standards. In "Life without Gadgets," Douglas offers a humorous account of life without modern conveniences. Although she fictionalizes details of her private life, including the adoption of children, the description of the daily round closely conforms to her own life.

"That," I observed cheerfully, "will certainly pull down the Canadian average." The census taker grunted noncommittally and I could see him straightening his face into deadpan.

The "that" referred to my answers to the questions for fifth houses: telephone? no; television? no; radio? no; vacuum cleaner? no (it looks like one, but it works like a carpet sweeper); electricity? no (gas and oil lamps); freezer? no (a beautiful root house instead); refrigerator? no (cooler); washer? no; ironer? no; bathroom? no; heating fuel? wood (in an oil drum heater); cooking fuel? wood (in a stove so old you can't get parts for it).

There was a lot more, but that will give you an idea. The enumerator (we didn't know each other; he came from a town) read back my answers as though they might change before his eyes. "Have you," he asked finally, "any running water at all?" Of course there wouldn't be running water, his tone said.

Oh, but there is. It's in the kitchen and it comes cold and delicious from well to stone storage tank to the shiniest of taps. The day something besides hope came out of that faucet was a gay day indeed. No more struggling up the rise from the well with buckets or washing vegetables in a pan. Not to mention the sudden ease of hand rinsing, tooth cleaning, kettle filling. I used to make special trips to the sink to gaze tenderly at that tap. If it had been there from the beginning would I have given it more than a casual glance?

Of course I wouldn't. Most of my life had been spent in modern houses and apartments which operated by finger-tip control and a toe-tickle for the sani-can. (Pardon me, the garbage disposal unit.) My early living and learning had been done in Montreal, Toronto, the United States, and until my father died I didn't know what pinching a penny meant. After that I found out, but still I was never—well, shall we call it "inconvenienced"? At 17 I was working on a farm (modern) and later I had all sorts of jobs: filing clerk, typist, shopping service, photographer, journalist, ad writer. By the time I married I was making good money and after that things were even better financially. Each new gadget I accepted as my right (even the built-in boredom) and whisked through housework and cooking like Mrs. Jehu. Each night I stretched out luxuriously in a long warm bath and thought I was one of the luckiest women in the world. I still do.

When I remarried (my first husband died), two children adopted in their teens were also married and far away. By this time I was living in British Columbia, where I am now. The simple reason for that move was that here I don't have hay fever and anywhere else I've been I have. Then I got to love the place and when I met my husband-to-be it seemed that we both had a city-smogged yen to "get away from it all," for a time at least. That time has stretched to 13 years—for me. The dark d's of distance and death have left me alone now.

"Alone" is not quite the word when summer comes and so do the visitors to these 140 acres on Cortes Island. The island lies between Campbell River and the mainland, about 100 miles north of Vancouver. It is 20 miles by 8 and resembles a pretzel with cramps. There are five small communities on it—the whole population isn't more than 500—of loggers, trollers, a few farmers, small cattle and sheep ranchers, artists, writers, retired people, and summer visitors. I thought I might join the writers, but during the last few years the spade has been mightier than the pen.

My first sight of the medium-size shake-roofed house which is my home was from a rowboat at black midnight after getting off the Union Steamship from Vancouver. If I had really wanted to see my hand in front of my face I would have had to use an infra-red spotlight. Suddenly the darkness whooshed. "What's that?" "Whale," said my husband. "Killer whale." "Whale! KILLER!"

It was quite an introduction to "Channel Rock" and I couldn't help contrasting the locomotion with my former push-button zooming through city streets. But acquaintance soon ripened into friendship and it wasn't long before anyone who came within yoo-hooing distance had to take a guided tour of main house, small stone cottage two bays over, barn, boat house, woodsheds, stone root cellar, and even what is coyly called "the little house." Only one neighbour has managed to evade me and visitors from outside haven't a hope.

The tour includes long vegetable rows, orchard, and holly trees, with flowers around all of them. There is a rockery in front of the house and just 20 feet above the sea that is filled with flowers from March to December. From the living-room you can see across the Straits of Georgia to the often snow-tipped mountains on Vancouver Island. In summer sunlit days or winter moonlit nights it's too beautiful for any words of mine. Not that everyone thinks so, however. One city visitor looked it over and then remarked:

"Can't say I care for it. Take away the sea and the mountains and what have you got?"

Well, you have the firs, hemlocks and cedars, which are quite something to see in these coastal forests. You have the trails through them; one of these runs for nearly two miles to the island's main road, meeting it at a point which is another mile from Whaletown: a small settlement of church, school, post office, store, library, clinic (a doctor flies in once a month; a dentist once a year) and homes which house about 50 families. Two miles along the road in the opposite direction is the community hall and another store. Channel Rock is really isolated and when the sea is too rough for a 9 foot boat the trail is the only way to get anywhere. In fact, you might say the whole island is isolated as we have had no regular passenger boat since 1953. Travel is by small plane or water taxi. Mail and supplies come in once a week on a freighter. No invitation "outside" is accepted without a "weather permitting" proviso.

Another trail winds from the house up through the woods for an eighth of a mile to a green gate in a long fence. Inside that fence, which the deer patrol

Channel Rock from the air, with Marina Island in the foreground.

Built on rock at the water's edge,
the cabin nestles into a cliff at its back.

Douglas dressed for the trail, 1950.

Store and dock in downtown Whaletown, 1950.

The cabin as it was in 1949, when Douglas moved there.

With no road access, Channel Rock can be reached only by foot, boat, or airplane.

The cabin from the cliff above.

*Christmas,
a favourite time
of year.*

*Corner of living-room,
late 1950s/early 1960s.*

*Living-room and
kitchen with barrel stove.*

Weather station, with a robin announcing spring.

*Douglas with
her fourth husband,
Philip Major Douglas,
in Vancouver.*

The many visions of home.

Frosty's kittens
peer down
from a shelf.

Douglas's animal neighbours
often became subjects
of her writing and photography.

The Church of St. John the Baptist in Whaletown, where Douglas gave the annual sermon on the World Day of Prayer for many years.

A red rose covers the side of the barn at the entrance to the garden at Channel Rock.

hopefully, is the farm end of things: chicken house, barn and the aforementioned food on the hoof. A mile on a winding trail brings you to the home of my nearest neighbour. Another neighbour is about the same distance away from the house in the opposite direction. I can't even answer as one farmer did when asked if his house had a good view:

"From the front porch you can see Ed Miller's barn, but beyond that there's only a bunch of mountains." The mountains are there all right, but not a building to be seen.

At Channel Rock the main house is some 40 years old and not too well insulated, but in a snowy winter like this last one the living-room with its beamed ceiling and half-panelled walls can be awfully cosy. The corner made by the oil drum heater, one of several built-in bookcases, and part of the kitchen wall is just the place for that big, round galvanized tub of steaming water which is now my bath. So first I'll answer a question that is looked but, so far, not asked: "Do you *really* feel clean with just that little tub and sponge baths?" (Note how relative size can be!)

Our great-grandparents—and, if we're old enough, our grandparents or even our parents—almost certainly spent at least part of their lives without benefit of bath tub. Would you say that they were never really clean? Hardly. Perhaps they were even cleaner than some of their descendants. They had to work harder at it and could never take it for granted. In some "uncivilized" homes I've known—including my own—baths were a daily affair, but some modern bath tubs operate on a once-a-week schedule.

While we're on this sanitary subject, let me say that most of the other homes on this island have everything Channel Rock hasn't in the way of mod cons. Those who live in them heat with oil, cook with propane gas, own speed boats, cars, telephones, television sets, washing machines, lighting plants; buy frozen food at the stores and keep their bathroomed house up-to-the-minute.

Now for the perennial "But whatever do you DO in that place?" The impossible problem is how to find time for everything. Pioneer living itself takes a bit longer: the difference between clicking a switch and wood-heating a stove; running down to the corner store or next door to a neighbour's compared to walking or boating for miles; getting fertilizer or fencing up to the barn by motor instead of shank's mare. . . .

High fashion and I were once as one, but now we're not even on speaking terms. One Sunday last winter I resembled nothing so much as a koala bear as I waddled down to my open boat for the two-and-a-half-mile ride through a heavy snowstorm to early communion. A pack on the back is a walking must for me at any time; high rubber boots are standard equipment except in summer. As I may suddenly take off from work on a bald eagle count or a harlequin survey or sniffing on the news of rare cougar or bear tracks, any photograph of me at such times would take first prize in the wildlife section.

From February to November the months are mainly filled with food production and selling, brush cutting, fir seed planting, gathering seaweed for fertilizer and bark for fires, visitors, canning, harvesting—and the 1001 extra jobs, on each of which nine stitches can be saved if it is done NOW. In winter the organizations are going full blast and daily chores never stop. This is also the season for all the indoor jobs you couldn't work into the rest of the year and getting wood ahead for next winter's heating. Time is always made for thinking, but now it is possible to catch up a bit on reading, talking, sewing, writing. Each spring half of a halcyon day goes into deciding what fertilizers, seeds, sprays should be ordered and if a chaperone will really keep pussies away from the petunias and WHAT will keep the deer from guzzling the ornamental cherry just two feet away from the living-room window. After that it is usually necessary to get the snow off the roof before warming air increases its weight another ton.

Question 3: Wouldn't such isolation make marriage more difficult? It depends on the marriage and that depends on the people who are in it. Any relationship is more difficult—if you want to put it that way—when there are no crowds, movies, television, shopping, job away from home, to act as buffers between the persons concerned. Two people see each other with much greater clarity—not always charity—and there is more opportunity for little habits to rub the wrong way. Marriages have been broken in isolation that might have continued with city cushioning. On the other hand, this simple, uncluttered living makes a good marriage better. People have to be themselves—and what wonderful depths of kindness, wisdom and laughter can be found in others when there is the space and time in which to do it.

Surely such a life would be hard on children? I've given a lot of thought and observation to that question and I'll have to answer it with the politician's: yes—and no. "Make over, make do, do without" are three seeds of such a life. They grow character. So does the dependency of each member of an isolated family upon the others. If you are any good at all you want to make their living safer. This is not an easy life: it is hard physically, mentally, morally. "Hard" is a bad word these days, but every single one of the really great men and women this world has ever known knew the value of that word and made it their own. Children find their circulation, their brain cells, their imagination and inventiveness stimulated by the emergencies of such a life and the necessity of providing their own entertainment. Each one has his own job to do and knows he is important in the home plan. "From each according to his ability, to each according to his need" is not a recent communist slogan but a way of life as old as the first smoke of the first pioneer.

When I say this life is hard morally I mean that it is easy to lapse into slipshod ways (Britons in jungles didn't dress for dinner just for the fun of it) and they can lead to worse things. Also, self-discipline is more of a must here than it is where close quarters do part of the schooling. Where there is little news, gossip can become a way of life. (Yet there is the other side of gossip too: a real interest in your neighbour's affairs.) I have heard of women on isolated farmsteads who would be friends, quarrel and make up again—all without seeing or speaking to each other. In isolation things have a tendency to become more than life-size.

I've never been able to see why walking a couple of miles to school (I used to do it myself) should be harder on children now than it ever was. Nor can I remember pushing a button because of the Joneses or status symbols. Yet I honour differing views and realise that, in an increasingly crowded world, my views are really the "different" ones. Children are particularly vulnerable to a public opinion that so labels them and marriages can founder on the rocks of "they say." But I remember with deep pleasure the city boy who hated work, discipline, responsibility, any life without gadgets, yet who became a man through these things he had once detested.

Now for the question that is asked most frequently: "What about illness or accident, when there is no doctor on the island and Channel Rock is so isolated?" You take your chances, as you do when you cross a city street or go down to the cellar (most accidents happen in the home and many of them in bathtubs!) or up with the jetliners. Surely no one still believes that this is a safe world?

Alone one November I caught cold after a drenching on my way to the community hall for a meeting which had been postponed, only I didn't know it. A couple of days later the wind began to slam from south-east to north-west and back to south-east again. In three weeks no boats went by and the trail was a mess of windfalls. At that time my nearest neighbour was in the community itself and anyone with any sense was staying close to home. In that decided isolation I managed to come down with, and partially recover from, the nicest little case of virus pneumonia that ever wheezed. At 103 degrees my hand shook the thermometer against the edge of the table and broke it. Which was just as well for my peace of mind. Nights were nightmares of sitting up gasping, with my heartbeat shaking the bed. Before I got lost altogether I vowed two things that will make you laugh: that I wouldn't fail to take the twice daily weather reading (I am weather observer for the island) or a sponge bath just as often. Evidently I took the weather, for the record's there, but otherwise two days disappeared completely from my lie. After that things improved and by the time people realised that no one had seen me lately I was still holding myself together when I coughed, but definitely on the mend. Later, letters from friends with the same virus convinced me that I'd been even luckier than I thought. One had picked up a jaundice infection while in hospital and two more reacted so badly to penicillin that they were weeks convalescing from that.

Believe me, I'm not advocating this life for everyone. There are good friends whom I've never asked up here because we both know they'd hate it. But I've tried to show in this story that it is a life which can be lived and lived happily, even by someone with little preparation for it. I'm not against progress; only against throwing away all the old things in favour of all new. Blended broth tastes so much better. There is a small transistor radio here now and except for the building and disposal difficulties (this house is on a rock jutting out into the sea and with a cliff close back on it) there would probably be a bathroom. But then what would the pussies do without a big toe rising from foot tub for them to bat? The boat has a 3 h.p. outboard and when electricity comes in, as it will before long, only the expense of getting it out this far will keep the bulbs from beaming at Channel Rock. Yet there are times when I do think of those all-electric families freezing and starving in the dark (to hear some of them tell it) when the power went off in Vancouver for a couple of days a few years ago. It's a sad thought and my heart bleeds for them. What am I saying? I was one of them once.[7]

Despite the humorous tone of this article, and despite Gilean's early attempts to lay down strict rules for the marriage, her first months on Cortes were extremely unhappy. Her journal from the fall of 1949 records her longing to be back in her beloved mountain valley. "How can there be such desire in anyone's heart and nothing come of it?" she mourned. "Whenever the scent of wet earth comes strongly to me then I am back in Home Wood again on my own lovely trails. Will I ever walk them again? I almost despair of it, but how can I live out my life like this—in this community place with people and boats and no walks that aren't uphill and such a shut-in feeling with the cliff behind? And the rocks! Such sterility everywhere instead of the good earth. If I were in the cottage it would be so much better. Earth around and more birds and quietness and aloneness. That is the way I want to live out my last days—not like this!"[8]

Especially oppressive was the lack of solitude. "This life is no life for me. Too much house, too many things around, too much routine and always the feeling that I have to be bright and gay for Phil and talk to him. I can't let him down, but how I long to live my own life again! The cottage would almost do it, but I feel that he has let me down there. He seems unable to understand how I feel about it."[9] Only when she was alone could she "almost feel a friendliness" for her new home.

As she had feared, her relationship with Phil deteriorated. "He says such nice things but he doesn't do what would give me happiness. He gets slower and slower and takes longer and longer to do things. Seven hours out of the day gone just in meals. It takes him an hour to prepare each one and sometimes more than an hour to do the dishes. And the cottage! I can hardly think about it without crying."[10]

EXILE END

Now I lie upon my bed
and the surfing sea sounds fade;
I am in the valley hut
that my heart and fingers made.

I am truth-sprung from the earth,
I am faith-fledged of a star,
light and shadow were my birth
where the crested mountain are.

Now I lie upon my bed
with the questing surf so near,
but farther than the tilting song
of the solitaire I hear.

Farther than the river stone,
farther than the forest tree,
and never heard above the lone
silence of tranquillity.

Now I lie upon my bed
where the wind is sand and foam,
my last breathing mountain-fled
on tansy air of home.[11]

Predictably, Douglas's homesickness for the mountains and her discontent with her marriage brought on another thyroid attack, probably exacerbated this time by menopause. By November, she had left for Vancouver. "I must get some help from the doctor. This terrific nervous tension, the pounding of my heart right up into my head, the dreadful exhaustion and all the awful rest of it have pretty nearly finished me in these last five months. I must have help or I will surely die."[12]

Once again, the medics advised surgery and predicted dire consequences without it. True to form, Douglas refused that advice and treated herself through her usual remedies: rest, quiet, and solitude. Throughout all these upheavals—the loss of her cabin, unhappiness with her marriage, severe health problems—she had continued to write and publish, but now the combination of factors was beginning to hamper her all-important work. "Except for articles on my beloved Valley, which I can always do, I have written nothing original for weeks. . . . Is even my work going back on me? It was my refuge and my strength; my ever-present help in time of trouble."[13]

REFUGEE

The haggard face of dawn, so still and grey,
Is pressed against my window. Go, dawn, go!
You were so kind to come this weary way,
But I must never hear the things you know,
Must never hear them. Look, dawn, look at me!
My eyes are sunken and my cheeks are wet
Because there is a road I cannot see,
Because there is a hill I must forget.
Touch me and go, while I shall bow my head
And tremble for the things you might have said.[14]

In her younger years, Gilean Douglas had sought both love and a career. Often the two were incompatible, but it was always the relationship and never her work that was abandoned. Writing had been the centre of her life since childhood and she could no more give it up than cease to breathe. The possibility that she would have to choose writing over marriage was becoming clearer, but Phil, for his part, was desperately trying to work out their problems and to find the happiness they both claimed to seek. Gilean spent the winter in Vancouver but returned to Cortes in the spring of 1950 to give the marriage another chance.

Upon her return to Cortes, Douglas launched herself into island life. Although small, the community was active, and she soon played a leading role. She joined the Women's Institute, the Women's Auxiliary to the Anglican Church, and the Whaletown Community Club and was immediately elected to office in all three. Once more her peers recognized her organizing drive, as had been the case from her earliest childhood endeavours with writing and dramatic productions. Douglas had a strong commitment to public service, but her community work also took her away from home and gave her the opportunity to be out in the world on her own.

Meanwhile, Major kept busy as president of the Gorge Hall Society and as a representative on the district school board. Life at Channel Rock staggered along, with gardens made and survival managed, but husband and wife avoided each other for much of the time through their community commitments and work. Yet Gilean's prediction that "I will keep driving you and you will hate it and eventually hate me" proved fatefully true, and she returned from a trip in November of 1953 to find that Phil had left for good.[15] Once more she stood alone and abandoned.

WARNING

Never say to one you love—
"Beauty lies
Where the marsh sleeps and the brown
Wood duck flies."

Never say to one you love—
"Share with me
In the tender whispering
Of this tree."

Life may suddenly grow dim—
Stars may fall.
Better not to ever say
This at all.[16]

Her first impulse was to flee Cortes. She doubted that she could do the heavy work of carrying firewood and water, working the garden, and packing supplies in and out over the long forest trail. As well, Whaletown had become even more isolated because boat service had dropped from two freighters and a passenger boat each week to only one small freighter. But Douglas feared leaving her house empty and her possessions unguarded and decided to remain for the winter while she sought a buyer for the property. But the land itself changed these plans.

SLOW WEATHER

This is the slow time of autumn weather:
days made for dreaming, nights made for sleep.
Here is the mist and a leaf and a feather,
here is the river, darkling and deep,
and the grey cords of rain to bind them together.[17]

During the next several years, Douglas made Channel Rock truly her own as she repainted her house, rebuilt several old sheds, and made many new plantings in the garden. Once more she reconstructed her life through nature and writing, and found a way of being that was to be hers for the next forty years. "The Protected Place," as she called it, offered her haven and solace, and once more a place, rather than a person, became the beloved. Living there by herself, Douglas found that the solitude of her home, her work in the community, and her writing combined to make a life well worth living.

CHAPTER **8**

Finding Home and Community

*H*er last marriage over, Gilean Douglas settled into an energetic routine of writing, community work, and all the chores entailed by her pioneer way of life. As she had in the mountains, she began a close study of the natural world surrounding her. She became a weather observer for the government in 1954, and twice a day recorded temperature, cloud cover, precipitation, and wind velocity from the weather station on the rock in front her cabin. She continued this daily routine until 1993. (Environment Canada formally recognized her extraordinary volunteer commitment with an award in 1983.) In Douglas's article "Winter Day," the conditions measured by her weather instruments— "Maximum temperature 21, minimum 18, cloud 10, wind force 5 with NE gusts to force 6, snowfall just over 5"—serve as the starting point for a reflective look at the observed details of a day.

A Bute wind is as bitter as trust betrayed. In the winters when it keens down its namesake inlet with snow on its breath there isn't a crack in my walls it doesn't blow through. In the attic it puffs up the insulation sheets and then slaps them down, so that they sound like sails doing too much abouting. As I drift off to sleep I could imagine that Channel Rock was away on a white sea voyage.

When I wake up, darkness is a black cat stretched across my world. No moon, no stars, only the lights of Vancouver Island like pale yellow eyes under a smut-browed sky. Looking out the window I see that the wind's temper fit has abated and the flat sea has a hard, steely look. Mountains hump wanly in icy air and pale trees seem huddled together against the snow which is surely coming again. The only sounds, within or without, are the small stirrings I make as I light an oil lamp against the chill dark and dress quickly in ski clothes.

It is 7 a.m., the time for the first of my twice-daily weather observations. When I open the door to go out I plunge into a knee-deep drift and have to stamp a path to the weather station. It must have snowed all night with the Bute wind whipping it into soufflés and meringues, plus a big baked Alaska which was once the miniature rose bed. The house roof has grown a white beard with long icicles hanging from it. Only a few weeks ago a frog trio sang in the pool and the rockery was a symphony of pinks and purples. Now the pool is a skating rink for Atcho, (Navaho for Catkin) Frosty's grandchild. Winter jasmine and Christmas roses are the only brave bloomers. No gull calls and the big loon swims silently across the bay, his white breast shining in the dark. I am wrapped in winter silence and loving every moment of this quiet prelude to the daily dozen plus.[1]

Douglas overcame her personal troubles and continued to write. Driven by the necessity of supporting the household when she and Phil Major moved to the island, and of supporting herself after his departure, she worked hard at selling articles, short stories, and poems to newspapers and magazines. In one year, for example, she sold 111 articles and short stories and 81 poems. Many of these articles looked back to the mountains for their inspiration, but she also began to write about coastal life and communities.

Through her work with the Women's Auxiliary of the Anglican Church, Douglas became friends with Canon Alan Greene of the Columbia Coast Mission. Founded in 1905 by John Antle, the CCM became the largest marine mission on the British Columbia coast. For more than sixty years it offered year-round, all-weather service for the medical, social, and spiritual needs of communities scattered from Sechelt to Cape Scott. The mission's fleet consisted of a travelling hospital ship, the *Columbia*, and a series of small ambulance ships.

When the mission ran an essay contest to publicize its work and raise funds, Douglas entered and won with an essay entitled "Saltchuck Salvation." The prize was a trip aboard the *Columbia*. This trip, which Douglas took in 1950, was the first of many adventures she would have on CCM vessels over the course of the decade. In effect, she became a sort of volunteer publicist, taking photos during her trips and producing articles that documented the mission's activities.

Douglas's research on the mission ships also led to a series of articles describing and celebrating life in the small coastal settlements. These articles, accompanied by her own photographs, highlight the details of daily experience, especially for those not usually documented—women and aboriginal peoples. As with her other works, these were marked by careful observation and engaging writing, but they also document a way of life which has disappeared along with many of the natural resources on which it was built.

Later, Douglas revised these articles as part of a planned book about coastal life and communities in the 1950s. Her eye and insight dwelt at length on the daily life of people on the coast, as evidenced in "Dock for Their Doorstep."

> Even on the British Columbia coast, which has just about everything, fish wives were few and far between in those days. I don't mean the woman who went out with her husband to flick flies at flighty fins when the dawn was cracking up. There were a number of those on this coast, as elsewhere. Nor the woman who used Billingsgate language, although there were several of them around too. But the woman who lived on a small gas boat for months on end, sometimes not putting a foot on land for weeks. Who ate, slept, cooked, and quarrelled with her husband in an abbreviated cabin with maybe an internal combustion engine in the middle of it. Who baked when the ship was rolling and hung her washing on fish lines. Her plumbing was a pail and she either hated the life or she loved it. . . .

> The deck of a thirty-foot salmon troller could be a maze of four fishing poles with their lines, two hand lines, gurdies, trolling leads, pulleys, davits, bobbers, stabilizers, pigs, flashers, spoons, bright-coloured threads to lure artistic fish— and all the rest of a troller's paraphernalia. Fishing was done from the cockpit, just astern of the fish running. Sometimes there was half a ton of ice in the hold—which was a good place for keeping vegetables when the fish didn't want it. The trunk cabin of the boat had the tail gunner's bubble from a fighter plane over it for a skylight. A dinghy was either being trailed or it stood upright on deck holding odds and ends protected by plastic covers. Down below was usually pretty crowded with a bunk, a gas stove for cooking, an oil stove for heating, a table, perhaps a chair. Every inch of the remaining space except a three foot square in the centre, would be taken up by a water tank and assorted cupboards. Radio, fan, and lights ran off a storage battery. Every boat that I saw differed in decor. Some looked positively luxurious while others were bare as a monk's cell. . . .

> On board some of these busy boats, there might be a "little breakfast" of coffee and toast an hour before daylight. "Big breakfast" with fruit, eggs, bacon, toast,

tea or coffee, could come between seven and nine depending on the time of year. Then lunch, afternoon tea, supper and a bedtime snack. Calm or blow, there was usually tea or coffee every two hours or so. If the fisherman smoked cigarettes his wife probably put one in his mouth when he wanted it and lighted it for him. When your hands are covered with fish blood and slime, you can't do things like that for yourself.

"The men need to eat a lot," said Shirley Walker. "Trolling is hard work, physically and mentally. When the fish are biting you haul them in until your arms ache and when they're not you ask yourself why until your head aches. You speed up and slow down, fish deep and fish shallow, check and recheck your gear—why in the name of Ogopogo aren't they biting? The first year I was married I no sooner finished one meal than I had to start another. But now I've got a system—and a pressure cooker."

When the stove has siderails on, the deck has the heaves, and everything not nailed down has the flying jitters, getting five meals a day and coffee every two hours isn't as simple as it sounds. In fact, you can even be in port and have catastrophes. You can bake a cake and put it in the oven just before five fishermen come to call and sit down together along the port gunwale. That cake came out of the cooker four inches high to port and half an inch high to starboard. . . .

Each spring careful couples did an overhaul job: caulking, copper painting, putting the engine in shape, rigging lines, checking gear. "If you didn't do a thorough job," said Jean, "the torredos that are all holding hands on the keel might let go and then the bottom would drop out." Some fish boats are pretty drab inside, others fairly sing with colours: gay curtains at the windows, sparkling linoleum on the floor. Red geraniums on a coffee table, scarlet counterpane on a double bunk, and scarlet pillow covers with white sailboats splashed across them. "In single bunk boats," put in Carol, "you and your husband have to make a duet of it when either one wants to turn over. You inhale by numbers and snores aren't allowed: they make you expand too much.[2]

On Cortes, Gilean was rooted in her garden, which provided sustenance for body and soul. In "Seeding by the Saltchuck," her sympathetic description of the makeshift gardens tilled by stranded women recognizes the salvation these efforts provided.

Nothing discourages green-fingered women. Even if their homes rest on planks laid across logs which go up and down with the tide over fathoms of saltchuck. Even if every teaspoonful of soil has to be dug out from between rocks on a perpendicular shore. Even if that soil has to be boat-carried in buckets to fill the boxes which are their only gardens. Their chickens can't scratch, their dogs can't bury bones, but almost every float wife on the British Columbia coast could and would grow flowers when I knew them.

On the Moore float in Moore Bay, some two hundred miles north of Vancouver, there was one Delft–blue and white house with a blue picket fence around it, flowers climbing over it, and window boxes burgeoning with bloom. When I was there a new house was being built, doors and windows had just been cut into the walls—and half a dozen window boxes were ready and waiting for sills to perch on. I caught a glimpse of them the next year as we sailed by and there was a flame of poppies and a matador's cloak of salvia against the red-gold of cedar, as though they had sprung out of a tree stump on a nearby mountain.

Window-boxes ranged from the usual sill variety to wooden troughs five feet long and half that wide or sometimes they were deep four-foot squares like giant seedling flats. There was excellent fertilizer all around: rotted wood from old fallen fir trees. When all the good timber had been taken out of one spot a tug would be called and the whole community of several houses and as many work buildings on each float would be towed to another location. Including the gardens. That's where saltchuck gardeners have it over others: they'll never have to dig up bulbs and precious plants just because it's moving day.

Seven miles west of Moore Bay is Cypress Cove. When Mrs. Hackett came up to live there with a married daughter who was an artist, she didn't stop at growing flowers. She also raised half a dozen different kinds of vegetables, and huge strawberries, all in long cedar boxes and an abandoned rowboat. She weeded and watered, sprayed and thinned as though her colourful boxes were large garden beds. The wood of these boxes was usually cedar as it lasts longer in a damp climate. Holes in the bottom insured drainage and copper painting the interior kept pests away. The mineral contents of the soil could be regulated much more easily than in the usual garden. Nasturtium, iris, phlox, poppy, aster and many other plants not only thrived, but often grew so tall they had to be staked. Mrs. Hackett was the widow of a British Army officer, with one son in Sandhurst and another in the Air Force. In Burma, where she was born, she could walk through miles of wild orchids. "But I like these northern plants even better," she told me. "Their perfume is so delicate and clean." She was very gentle, very quiet, very sure and a lover of solitude. The happiest hours of her day were when she was working with her growing things and could see them backgrounded by the lovely and lonely upcoast waters and mountains.

Working with flowers was sometimes just about all that saved the sanity of women who didn't like being floaters in the wilderness. Even their houses were models of modernity; a TV aerial sprouted from every roof and more frequent plane service had brought shopping centres closer. I watched one attractive young wife digging literally for dear life in a three foot long flower box. "Would you send me some plants?" she asked eagerly. "If I couldn't keep trying new things and planning I'd go crazy." On her next trip to that particular float, the *Columbia* carried flowers from my garden in half a dozen cedar boxes, all different.[3]

The trips aboard the mission boats offered Douglas new material for her writing and new topics for investigation. She was an excellent researcher who brought facts to life with her keen personal observation. "Best Port in a Storm" combines her look at life on an isolated coastal radio station with an introduction to the natural environment and abundant sea life of the location.

When the Sound began to look perpendicular we left Shushartie Bay in a hurry. The last thing we saw was the man who didn't like strangers, waving genially to us, which heartened me for the dusting we took crossing to Hope Island—eight miles long by half that wide—opposite the centre of Vancouver Island's north shore. Hope is well named. Its south shore is cut deeply by an inlet and that's where we turned. Once inside I felt as though I had suddenly gone deaf. The roar of the waves was only an echo and the deep channel through which we were sailing was as calm as any swimmin' hole. Rocky, evergreened cliffs sheered up on either side, closing in more and more until there seemed to be barely room for our big ship to slide by. But once through this narrow pass the channel opened out to a fair-sized bay where fishing boats, clustered around cannery scows, became identical twins in the mirror water. This was Bull Harbour, known to all coast cruisers as the finest shelter in those parts.

The stillness was uncanny. The wild call of a loon seemed to accentuate the silence. There was not even the trumpeting of sea lion bulls for which this harbour was named. Not that the sea lions weren't present. Once when our skipper, George MacDonald, was doing a little job of painting minus wind and wave, he looked up to see more than a hundred of them clustered around the ship. The Gillelands, who lived at the Bull Harbour government radio station, were almost wrecked in their dinghy one day when a big bull sea lion surfaced too close for comfort.

The radio station, with its tall masts and low white houses, has sheltering Bull Harbour on one side and the open reaches of what is practically the Pacific Ocean on the other. This exposed beach is called Roller Bay because the big combers coming in on an ebb tide roll the stones on it. It's a noisy sea song and when the Gillelands first came they could hardly sleep while it was going on. Now they never hear it unless they listen purposely. "But I guess we'll have to put an anchor on the island soon!" laughs Gordon Gilleland, who was in charge of the station. "That might be almost too true to be funny. Look over there, where the sea is driving that determined wedge into the land just beside the Station and our home!" I looked and it certainly seemed as though the ocean wanted to cut Hope in two. In a bad storm the whole island shakes.

Those storms can be magnificent or terrifying, depending on how you feel about storms. In one blow a sixty foot fir with a five foot butt was driven from the water into the salal brush far up on land, while lesser trees snapped off like twigs. Storms like that keep everyone from sleeping and all along the shore dead trees, saltwater-killed, rattle in the wind. . . .

"Sunset and a ship's wake at Bull Harbour."

A COASTAL
ALBUM
*Douglas's
photographs
document life
in remote
settlements of
coastal British
Columbia
in the early
1950s—a way
of life that has
now vanished.*

l to r: *Canon Alan
Greene, John Young,
and Rev. Heber Greene,
Kingcome Inlet, 1950.*

The Wahkana Bay *at dock in Whaletown.*

Ken Slater, skipper of the
Wahkana Bay.

A patient being slung
aboard a mission boat.

"The second Columbia *tied up at a floating logging camp in beautiful Knight Inlet. When it's rough enough you can be seasick right in your own living-room."*

"The cold, grey dawn of a winter morning on Knight Inlet."

At a float camp in Seymour Inlet, 1950.

"Float children have play pens to keep them away from the water."

"The float home of a logger and his family where the Columbia *has paid many a visit."*

"The CCM hospital ships have visited lone loggers for 63 years."

The CCM hospital ship Columbia *docked at Whaletown.*

"Dr. W. J. MacTavish thinks out a medical problem in the Columbia's *surgery."*

*Luke Kingery of Seymour Inlet
with Jim, his pet crow, 1950.*

*Rev. Heber Greene
at a christening, 1950.*

*"A typical coastal logging camp
of Seymour Inlet, British Columbia.
Everything on floats."*

*Three loggers
and a cedar giant,
Knight Inlet, 1950.*

"Douglas fir coming out of Pacific coast forests."

Residents of the Dot Logging Camp in the valley of the Klinaklini River, Knight Inlet, 1950.

Son of one of the teachers at an upcoast Indian village.

Interior of the church at
Kingcome Inlet.

Dick Flanders and his grandchild
Louise at Mamalillaculla,
Village Island, 1950.

"The flags are flying at Kingcome Indian village. Canon Alan Greene
inspecting the machine that makes them fly."—1950

In some ways life at Bull Harbour was much the same as in other small communities. The men stood their watches, serviced the installations, worked in their gardens. The women gardened too, looked after home and children, gave tea parties, studied mail order catalogues, read and visited each other. But the isolation out of fishing season was very different from that of the average rural community. Except for the La'Lasiquela Indian village some miles to the east, the station people were the only Hope inhabitants. If there was a storm outside that was too big for a fish boat to handle, they stayed put. Unless the *Columbia* happened to be around. She called in regularly every few weeks and in case of illness could be reached by radiophone.

But in fishing season the Gillelands and their neighbours could have all the company they wanted. Literally hundreds of boats—seiners, gill-netters and trollers—have been anchored in the harbour at one time and by night this widening of a remote inlet driven in to a tiny island looked like a neoned town. There was always someone talking, singing or just plain cussing. Engines started up and stopped again. The store and the coffee bar, connected with one of the two fish scows, did a roaring business. Salmon, halibut, hake, rock and ling cod, herring—they were all there for the buying—but salmon was king.

"Even if Bull Harbour was cut off from the rest of the world," said Gordon, "none of us would need to starve. There are always fish. In 1944 there were so many that they brushed against our legs when we went swimming. That season there were 283 boats in the harbour at once and 511 landings in a single season. The island mink have gone in for salmon and if they could get at the 6"–8" crabs they'd gulp with joy."[4]

While her journalism continued to pay the bills and generate wider and wider audiences, Douglas was also collecting her work into volumes. The fifties saw the first of her books come into print. She already had a modest reputation as a poet, and now she had the time to reflect on this work and draw it together into her first book of poetry, *Now the Green Word*. Published in 1952, this was followed the next year by a second book of poems (satiric verse), *Poetic Plush*. Just as significant as these works was the publication in 1953 of her first volume of nature writing, *River for My Sidewalk*. These recollections of her mountain home recreated and celebrated that lost paradise and her life in it. The rub was that the publisher believed no reader would accept the book as the work of a woman and so it was published under the pseudonym Grant Madison.

With the release of these major works, Douglas's readership expanded. She always maintained that, even alone, she belonged to a community through her writing, and her writing style always implies and often addresses the reader. In "The World Belongs to Cool Enthusiasts," she put this thought directly: "I do sit down and I do think and I do try to put those thoughts on paper in such a way that they can be helpful to someone else too. I know only a very few of the people who read my [writing] . . . so I have to imagine the others. I hope I'm not far off the target in my thoughts."[5]

Among Douglas's readers were friends who received her yearly Christmas letter. Begun in the early fifties, these annual summaries of life at Channel Rock were issued to a community numbering in the hundreds, and Douglas hand-wrote an extra, personal note on almost every one. She was an avid and faithful correspondent who lived many of her most intimate relationships in letters and maintained long-standing friendships through the mail. She had not seen many of her correspondents for years, and others she had never met in person, yet all of them remained vital parts of her social network. Gilean Douglas's life centred on Cortes Island, but her world extended far beyond it.

Douglas was just as busy with community work as with her professional and social writing. As an officer in the Women's Auxiliary of the Anglican Church, one of her main duties was to give the annual sermon on the World Day of Prayer. She first did this in 1952 and continued for the next twenty-two years.

Her most important involvement was with the Women's Institutes. Established by Adelaide Hoodless in 1897, the WI was the sister organization to the Farmers' Institutes and it sought to foster the skills of rural women, improve their lives and work, and celebrate their achievements. In the political arena, it fought for the education of women and, at home, helped communities improve the quality of life. On the island, the WI worked for local improvement. The Cortes chapter, with an active membership of about fifteen women, was ambitious and took on four major projects in 1952 alone: refurbishing the old cemetery, presenting a library to the school, raising funds to build a playground at the school, and financing the purchase of firefighting equipment.

In addition to local membership, Douglas served on the provincial and national boards of the WI. This commitment involved representing the organization at meetings across the country and writing articles about it that were published in newspapers and journals across Canada. Much of her time and writing skill was absorbed by these tasks, and for a while her own poetry and creative prose took second place to the WI responsibilities. Because of her creativity and considerable organizational skills, she was selected by the officers of the British Columbian WI to edit *Modern Pioneers,* a book to celebrate the fiftieth anniversary of the organization. Her work included writing the article on Cortes, collecting other articles from locals across the province, editing the submissions, and seeing the book through production.

Although Douglas's community work meant she had less time for her creative writing, she could not abandon her obligations. As a child of upper-class parents at the beginning of the twentieth century, she was bred to an ethic of public service and responsibility. Her sense of duty to community had always been strong, but on Cortes she found a place where it could find full expression. In her 1961 Christmas letter, she tried to explain her need to serve.

> These organizations are my community work: the means by which I can, in my small way, help neighbours, country and world. Yes, I know there are many others who can do these jobs as well and better than I, but I felt they were offered to me because what I had to give was needed in that place at that time. I have tried to answer that need with my best: for love, not lucre. . . . This community work seemed so necessary that I have made sacrifices—and believe me they were sacrifices, especially sometimes!—of time, energy and money for it. I have never regretted them; only wished I had more to give.
>
> All this I tell my questioning friends, but still they ask: "Couldn't you help more people if you concentrated on your writing?" . . . I don't know. I only know that I have done what seemed to need doing by me. That I have also tried—when speaking to a group or just with one person—to leave something of myself with them: something of inspiration and of love. When interviewing people or reporting news, I have put down the good I found in persons and events. To build, not destroy; to help, not hinder; to love, not hate; that is my creed. If it sounds too good to be true, forgive me. It has evolved from foolishness and mistakes and misunderstandings; from faults and failings which are still present, though I hope they are less than they were."[6]

By the end of the 1950s, Douglas's work on her own property and dedication to the life of the community had made Cortes her own. In putting down roots, she came to see herself as the inheritor of a long

Douglas in Vancouver, 1955.

Douglas (left) and other members of the Whaletown Women's Institute in front of her cabin, 1950.

*Petroglyph on a
beach boulder near
Manson's Landing
on Cortes Island.*

*Douglas on the steps
cut into the rock in front
of the weather station, 1950.*

Douglas (front row, fourth from left) attending a hospital opening in Quesnel as a representative of the Women's Institute, c. 1958.

Douglas (left) in Vancouver, late 1950s.

"Gilean Douglas of Whaletown, B.C.,
editor of 'Modern Pioneers,'
a history of British Columbia Women's Institutes."
PUBLICITY PHOTO FOR THE BOOK

history of habitation of the island. In the opening chapter to her later memoir of island life, *The Protected Place,* she recollects her finding and making of home and acknowledges those who came before.

THREE COME HOME

All day, the Union Steamship *Cardena* had been sailing up the Inland Passage from Vancouver. She moved rather majestically and with no hint of hurry. Up inlets, into bays, tying up now and then to docks she dwarfed by her presence. The sea was calm as certainty and with every mile north the air seemed clearer, the sunshine brighter. There were perhaps twenty passengers aboard. All of them relaxed on deck in warmth and timelessness. I was one of them. I was going to an island I had never seen where I had bought a home.

The sky flamed ochre and with that yellow Indians call "the colour of the west." One star came out in a clear sky, then millions of them. The ship's keel cut into black water and immediately it became silver, bubbling like champagne where touched. Now each small wharf we approached seemed lit by fireflies: points of light which dipped and rose and moved at all speeds, in all directions. When our deck lights came on we could see that the fireflies were flashlights held by the people waiting for us on the dock.

The dock was an oasis in the darkness of the surrounding forest with its little clearings. Voices—perhaps louder than need be—were thrown against the silence of land and sea. Winches skirted, freight landed with a thud and was manhandled into a shed. One or two passengers walked down the gangplank and were hailed by neighbours. The postmaster trundled a wheel-barrow of mail up to the tiny post office. Then the *Cardena's* engines throbbed, the gangplank was drawn in, the ship backed away cautiously and the upturned faces receded. Our deck lights went out and night closed in on the sea. On the shore the fireflies scattered in all directions.

It was after midnight when we made the port of Cortes Island where I had bought my home. I had three miles still to go, this time in a small boat with an inboard motor. After the *Cardena* pulled out, my guide and I walked down a steep gangplank to a swaying flat. Outlined in silver phosphorescence, we putt-putted into the silent dark.

I was silent too. I was feeling so intensely that my nerve ends were like fingers, groping for, touching, exploring this strange country where I was to live. Suddenly there were tremendous splashings not far away, where Marina Island should be by my maps and reckoning. Yes, there was the channel light.

"What's that splashing?" I asked.

"Killer whales."

Killer whales! What did they kill that other whales didn't? But a few moments later I had forgotten them in a sudden upsurge of contentment for which I could find no reason. Yet it stayed with me and even increased as we ran in below a high, huge rock from which a house seemed to be growing, dim in the starlight. Struggling up the long, stony, slanting beach I found a path behind the boathouse and followed it to my back door. I could hardly wait to get there.

Lifting the latch I walked into a kitchen where none of the cupboards had doors and there was only a hole where a sink and perhaps a water tap had been. This room led into a much larger one, half-panelled in dark-stained wood, with a beamed ceiling, a medium-size window, two French doors and a window-seat fronting on the sea. By starlight and flashlight I could see that the room was bare except for a wall of built-in bookcases, a large, homemade table and what looked like a camp-bed frame of wood and chicken wire webbed with deer thongs. Paper and a few books littered the floor. One door had a broken pane of glass near the slide bolt. It should all have been chilly and desolate, but I felt strangely warmed and comforted. I slept deeply on the camp bed in the sleeping-bag I had brought with me. It seemed as though I had come home again.

The feeling persisted next morning when I went out to explore: following a path to the well-house and chicken run near the beach, then the climbing trail which led to a root-house and finally to a barn and old orchard. The bracken was higher than my head and alders had shot up everywhere. A small stream beyond the orchard was choked with weeds and grass. Deer had broken down the fence which surrounded this farmland. Walking south along the fence line I came to a little bay where there was a half-finished cottage with an elfin, English look.

Everywhere I went I felt myself among friends and I knew that this was a place which had been deeply loved. All had been built with care and caring: the stone walls and paths, the three sets of stone steps where boats could anchor, the house, the trails, the out-buildings. The property had been vacant for nine years, but everything stood sturdily. On the trail from the cottage I found two great firs, 18'6" and 21'6" in circumference and a huge cedar measuring 22'5½" round. With gorgeous knees! Also a snag back of the barn which was 21'3" in girth and a fir down near the house which was only a little tree at 15'1".

The books I had seen that first night were now on my shelves: Burton, Borrow, Gibbon, Pater, Darwin, Tacitus, Gogol, Chatrain and several volumes on botany. Armed with Henry's *Flora of Southern British Columbia*—well marked by John Pool, who had owned the books and pre-empted the property—I began to explore the out-trails. It was then I became conscious of some rather odd happenings.

That inner feeling of happiness which never left me when I was at home— especially outside the house—now seemed to dim or brighten depending on where I was. Gradually it was borne in on me that on the trail to the road my spirits fell or lifted at the same place—about halfway—depending on which direction I was going. It was not far from the heronry. Yet on the south-east trail which led to The Gorge all was bright, all the way. When I climbed the cliffs and could look down on the channel where the geese congregated I was happiest of all.

One day a young fisherman and his wife came to see me, not for the first time. While we were having coffee, this rather prosy and practical man said, "There are dark places on this island. Sometimes it gets so bad that I have to jump into my boat and head out to sea. When I get beyond a certain point everything is all right again—until I start back. Have you noticed anything like that in your boat or on the trail?"

"Yes," I said and then: "Is this one of the dark places?" But I was sure it was not.

"No, no," he answered and his rather serious face broke into the nicest smile. "I feel just fine here. Somewhere on your trail it begins, a sort of darkness, but this is a place where there is light." From him this was sheer poetry.

So then I had more to think about and how I longed for John and Elizabeth Pool to come back and tell me what they had felt about this island. That they had kept much to themselves I knew and that John had built a second trail, which bypassed the house, between The Gorge and the road. Had this anything to do with the "darkness?"

Four friends who came after the fisherman had left the island mentioned the strange feeling they had at a certain part of the main trail and they photographed the place. It was where I felt "strange" too. One or two others have told me something of the sort, but many people are reluctant to speak of such things in case they are thought weird.

I had heard of the old Indian wars in this district, of the measles and smallpox which swept over the island after the white man came. Could these cause the "darkness?" I thought of Dunsany's poet, walking, centuries later, over a forgotten battlefield and knowing it for what it was.

There were middens and old encampments of the Slaiaman on Cortes. Today, the Squirrel Cove band of the Klahuse from Toba Inlet lives on the east coast of the island. Their name for The Gorge entrance is *Yippaco*—"ice shatters (bow of canoe)." We have little now of that sharp, thin ice which can break bows. Perhaps it was colder then.

When I started to dig over ground at the side of the house I found that I was digging clamshells. Probably seal hunters had been in the habit of stopping here, or small bands on long voyages. Primitive canoe bays can be seen in my cove and in two other coves nearby. Who had come in the long ago past to this place I called Channel Rock? For I felt myself an inheritor, a custodian, as far as possible, of what had been. . . .

"It is done. The dream is on the rock. The dream is for always. The sun which is for always was the dream. As a learner of medicine, as a maker of medicine, I prayed to the sun. I prayed to the Great Spirit through the sun. I am Kwelte-sqet, named after the red clouds of sunrise and sunset. Now the sun has guided my fingers to paint my dream: the sun on the rock. It is done. It is good."

Facing the south, but swaying first east, then west, he sang the song which had been given him in his dream. Then the dance spirit came on him. Between the rock and the arbutus trees he danced. To the sun of the sunrise, to the sun of the sunset, to the way between, to the feet on that way, he danced. "It was all in the dream, it is all on the rock. It has been, it is now, it will come," he sang as he danced.

Suddenly it was over and he was empty. Nine lights and nine darknesses it had been, the cleansing and the fasting; the drinking of sea water, the bathing to the four winds and rubbing with seaweed; the beating with fir branches, the woods-wandering and praying. Then the dream and the painting. He had chewed salmon eggs to stir in stone with stone. He had not swallowed them. He had mixed them with his spit and spat them into the red clay, which had been ground into powder the colour of sunrise, the colour of sunset.

He had other paints in the pouches of deer hide hung from the deer thong knotted around his waist. Yellow clay, black charcoal, the white of burned bone. But he had used only the red, the colour of life and luck and of the sun, smearing with dried fish skins to bind it to the rock. Now the colour was on his fingers which had made the painting. The colour was in the sparks which flew from the maple stick he twirled over cedar dust in a small maple bowl.

He had gone down to the shallow sleeping cave to make a fire. It was the Moon When the Birds Come Back and not cold, but the fire helped fill his emptiness. He squatted beside it, a long man, lean of body and head with an aquiline nose. Naked except for the thong and pouches. No shell or bone ornaments in nose or ears; no paint on face or body. His long dark hair, without grease or ochre in it, was caught back at the neck with a band of cedar. And he was hungry as he had not been for days. He found some bulbs and roots he had saved and munched them slowly, looking east to the mountains.

He knew about those mountains. His father had been there in his adolescent dream. "The mountain peaks talked to each other. Their voices sounded like bells," his father had said. "I walk about where the mountains are talking" was the way his dream song began. All his father's songs had come from wind and waves, mountain and stream, birds and wild animals. Grandfather had declared the whole family protected by Raven. That was why they had come to an island, for all islands are pebbles dropped by Raven.

Between the cave and the mountains the water was still, but the air drummed with wings. Great flocks of geese rested and fed in the channel. Thousands of ducks had come down by the Island-That-Grows-Longer. On the island where he was now there were many animals and birds. The sea was full of fish, its shores thick with good things to eat. Here the food dish was never empty. Not as it had been where Grandfather was born, where every moment of warmth must be spent in food gathering, so they would not starve in the cold-of-the-long-darkness.

He put more sticks on the fire and thought again of Grandfather, with his braided hair and his face like the west wind, proud and wise and kind. His grandfather spoke of the Homeland, where the white down of the sky buried everything except the smoke holes of the *kekules.* Then those coming in that only way must cry "A'la!" so the women could cover the food from soot and soil. Grandfather remembered being picked up from sleep as a small boy and hurled into devil's club for protection when raiders came. It was after that that his family and others of their blood fled down the Great River to the bitter water. But too many others were there. So they travelled towards the snow wind and built their slant-roofed cedar houses by the Sea-That-Is-Inside.

There he had been born and near that place he had found his guardian spirit. Later, it had come to him in a dream that he, who had never painted, except his skin with clay, charcoal and deer tallow, must paint on the rocks. So he took the red clay with him, mixed it with fish oil and tried it on an open rock by the beach. The colour was good. He had put two flicker feathers in his headband of cedar and let his guardian spirit guide his hand. He painted his guardian spirit, the Killer Whale. He painted the otter and wood thrush, his childhood playmates; his grandfather too and the way he had led them to this island. He painted until he was a skin bag full of nothing, until he did not know if he was awake or asleep. He had painted the spirit of the sun over it all, from the Sea-That-Is-Inside to where the geese come, then all the way round to the big rock and on to where the herons nest.

He would be a medicine man of the sun and young boys would come to follow him and learn. They would live together like the south wind. They would heal with the spirit stone and with the roots and herbs the wise women knew about. They would heal with the sun. They would have no slaves, sacrifice no animals, start no wars. They would not make fools of the sick or cure them only for gain, as some did. It would be a place of peace. Those who knew the sun would know that too: all those who would come here, now or after he had gone to the sun himself. He, Kwelte-sqet, who belonged to the Ocean People and to the Above People.

But now the shadows were growing longer and there was still much to be done. He must walk around all of this protected place. "Friend," he would say to each tree; "Honoured one," to each animal. Even the stones and grass he would tell about it. "It was all in the dream. It is all on the rock. It has been, it is now, it will come," he sang on the trail. . . .

The First World War, the war to end all wars, was over and the men of Cortes Island had come home again, those who could come home. Among them was John Pool: lean, medium-tall, medium-fair, deliberate in speech and action. He had built dry-stone walls in the county of York in England, taught school in Liverpool, married before taking on the job of school inspector in Boporo, Sierra Leone. Then he had come to Qualicum and finally to this Georgia Strait island to build a log cabin in The Gorge before joining the Army Medical Corps.

While he was away his tiny wife, Elizabeth, kept the home fires burning in the beachstone fireplace.

Now it was March of an early spring and John was rowing through the channel between Cortes and that island the Indians had called *Chamadaska*. Before that they had called it something else; a word—he had forgotten the Indian name old Qualicum Tom had told him—which meant island-that-stretches or something of the sort. The stretch would be the reefs, he supposed. The Spaniards under Quadra had named it "Marina" and described it as "nestling under the shoulder of Cortes." But the British Admiralty, shocked that it should ever have borne the name of the Mexican mistress of the Spanish *conquistador*, renamed it Mary. In 1906 the Canadian government declared: "In the beginning the name of this island was Marina and Marina it shall remain." This would be done, they said "in the interests of historical accuracy." But the oldtimers still called it Mary. "Don't hug Mary too close," they would tell you, looking at Shark Spit and the reefs.

Resting on his oars below a big rock jutting into the sea on Cortes, John thought he had never seen so many waterfowl as early as this. The whistling, sliding, bowing birds gave him a sense of comradeship and contentment. There was a comforting feeling about the whole place. A protected feeling—though he couldn't think why the word had come to him. It was too tame. A word for neighbours all around, afternoon tea on delicate china brought from England, four walls closing in—the sort of thing Elizabeth liked. Not this great sweep of sea and sky before him now with no house to be seen by day, no light by night except the steady channel marker with its big kerosene lantern. A forest of big trees and little underbrush, though loggers had gone through in 1915. No doubt there were cougar, bear, a few wolves left from the packs which used to roam the island. Protected? He laughed to himself. But the word stayed with him.

So did the thought of this place, where the sea-fowl gathered, eagles and herons nested, otters had a slide, many birds sang and the corydalis bloomed. Corydalis. That would be a good name for a house. For a house built on that big rock where it would be sheltered from the winter south-easters and the bitter Butes, with a bay on each side and its face to the great mountains rolling across Vancouver Island to the open sea. Allen Robertson had a pre-emption on the property, but perhaps he would release it. There would be shoreline and bays, a brook and a spring. In one bay there were the ashes of the split-shake cabin Bill Robertson had built there. Now the Dominicks from Squirrel Cove had a lean-to on the small tidal island to the north-west, to use when they were seal hunting off Mary. That was good. They fitted into the place.

So it was done. Allen Robertson's bride, Dorothy, had not wanted to live in such an isolated spot, where children might fall from the great rock. They had settled in the small community of Whaletown and John Pool began to build, slowly and deliberately and well. Trees were felled and logs cut to be towed by Joe Gregson and his troller to Eckhardt's mill on Read Island, later to be made into floors, ceiling beams and wainscoting. Shakes were split out of big cedars for roofs and outside walls. Timmy, the Pools' young brown horse which drew their democrat, was brought in over a deer trail to haul a stoneboat. Hundreds of rocks were needed for the root-house walls and the foundations of all the buildings. Though water was no problem, a well must be dug and cribbed between the house and the chicken run. Timmy lodged in the woodshed now, but there would be a barn for him and for Luci, (short for Lucifer) the cow.

At first John rowed to Corydalis from The Gorge, that almost-enclosed arm of the sea spreading out from a narrow entrance. Then he began to stay overnight in the woodshed when it was completed. Finally, when the new house itself had roof and walls, he moved in. By then he was cutting landing steps, three sets of them, up to the top of the big rock and building a stone reservoir. Like any good stone-waller, he disliked cutting his stones, although he had to do this many times. He travelled to all the nearby beaches and to Marina Island to find the rocks of different sizes that he needed. With his waller's hammer he knocked off knobs and comers from these, so the finished work would look neat and even.

For walls and storage tank he first marked out a base-line lengthwise, with string stretched between posts as a guide. Then a shallow trench was cut for the foundation stones. These stones must be as large and flat as possible. Walls were a little wider at the base than at the top and when built halfway up, large, flattish stones called "tie-stones" were inserted at intervals all the way along. These held everything together and gave the wall strength. From that point on John, being a meticulous workman, tilted his stones a small bit downwards from the centre, so the rain would run off and the walls last longer. At the top he laid a row of flat stones. As he was not fencing a field he did not bother with capping stones, but he spent many hours hammering or pressing in pebbles and small rocks to fill all spaces and keep the rain from deteriorating his good work.

In spite of all this hard labour, there was never a day when he did not walk through the forest or climb the cliffs looking for new birds and flowers. To hear John Pool and Bernie Allen discoursing on a flower was "like a mental minuet" said a neighbour in The Gorge. Some days the Gregsons came in to Corydalis by boat from their logging camp on Plunger Pass. Bob MacGregor, the prospector, walked down from Carrington Bay. Henry Saunders, the McLeans, the Kendricks, the Tookers, Harry Middleton, Donal MacDonald (who was said to be in with the James gang), Bill Robertson who kept the store and Thompson, the road foreman, all came by, and other neighbours gave a hand when needed. The Columbia Coast Mission ships, with John Antle and Alan Greene as skipper-chaplains, dropped anchor periodically below the big rock. John was a controversial man, so he had both enemies and friends. "He was a good friend himself," said Neal Carter, who stayed with the Pools in The Gorge when he was seventeen.

It was John and Timmy who did the bulk of the building and John liked it that way. More and more he wanted to stay at Corydalis. Just walking to the road he felt depressed the farther he got away from the place he now thought of as home. But always when coming back again he began to sing halfway, and always hymns. He didn't know why, for he hadn't been to church in years. "Art thou weary, art thou languid, art thou sore distressed?" He was none of these.

The big main room in the house had been partitioned off for a bedroom and the same in the attic, when the log cabin in The Gorge burned down and Elizabeth came to Corydalis to live. A little furniture had been saved and the china and some ornaments. John quickly threw up a lean-to with tongue and groove to be divided into kitchen, storeroom and small bedroom. But this meticulous workman wasn't happy with it. Elizabeth wasn't happy either. There was no insulation. The wind howled through the open-ended attic. She missed her cosy cabin and the lovely, old-fashioned garden which was "like a fairy tale told by moonlight," a poetic islander said.

But with the same courage which had enabled her to take long canoe trips with her husband into the West African interior, she faced this north-west wilderness. Shrubs and bulbs, slips and roots, were brought from The Gorge and replanted at Corydalis. This wild place bloomed into ordered English beauty. Her husband had finished the barn, cleared and fenced vegetable and grain fields, planted an orchard, built two large chicken houses and a fenced run to the beach for fifty fowl. As they were both vegetarians, eggs and milk were important. So Luci, the cow, had come to Corydalis with Elizabeth. On that trip Luci and John had made a spring song worth remembering.

Luci did well when driven down the open road but as she was used to a field, the forest spooked her. John and Jean Brisson pushed and pulled but she wouldn't budge forward. Then John, deciding the devil or his equivalent was in the cow, began booming out hymns; at once, Luci moved along the trail, mooing as she went. This continued for the mile and a half home. When they arrived John was croaking hoarse, but Luci continued her spring song in fine voice.

By this time the deer trail to the road and an Indian trail to John Lyle's home at The Gorge had been swamped out. Another deer trail led to The Gorge and the Indian paintings on the cliff. This was John Pool's favourite walk. He felt happy when he was on it, that deep, quiet happiness which was part of the man. Looking down at The Gorge he wondered if the Indians had ever called it the equivalent of "the place that grows bigger." That was what the bottleneck entrance expanding into a large "lake" looked like. He had asked the Dominicks, but they had only shaken their heads and smiled. Johnny said the entrance had a name—John couldn't pronounce it—which described what might happen to a boat running out into ice. How expressive the Indian languages were. How clearly and cleverly they saw things.

With fifty chickens, milk from Luci, miner's lettuce and other wild plants and the big garden and orchard, the Pools were self-sustaining. There was enough left over for sale to fill half the Whaletown dock on boat day, in that era of low freight rates to Vancouver. John traded some of his half-section of land: a beautiful, deep bay.

Beside the front door of his new home a lodgepole pine, shaped like a parasol, shaded part of the silver-shake house from the blazing sun of summer. The west rooms were painted dark green for added coolness. There were a bay window and a smaller one and two French doors. The new kitchen was grey with a scrubbed board floor, many-doored cupboards, a sink and small stove. Now the oil drum heater on the stone slab in the living room could be used for heating only. In the nearby bookcases were Pater, Gibbon, Gogol, Darwin, Burton, Borrow, Chatrain, Tacitus, several volumes on ancient and modern Egypt, many natural history books and hundreds more. John Pool sat reading them on winter evenings and was utterly content. Back and forth through his own gates cut in the outside doors went Felis, the black cat. Their little white Spitz had been left behind with neighbours in The Gorge.

Felis and John were up at first light in all seasons. In time to see Marshall Dominick paddle silently past the house in his dugout canoe on the way to Mary Island. In time to hear the dawn duck-talk as the flocks swept in from or took off towards the western mountains in migration. Sometimes he and Felis went to a cavern John had found one rainy day, with a blackened roof and the remains of old fires in it. From there they watched killer whales lunge up from the south and geese climb the morning. They had even slept there. It was the most peaceful place John had ever known. He wondered who had slept there before him.

Now he was working at the things he had not had time to do before: putting in a pool with water lilies, constructing more stone steps, making a bench with a log foot-rest where Elizabeth could watch the sunset on the sea, walling off for her what she called The Secret Garden. He took many photographs, developing his films in the kitchen where he had put in a cold water tap. He sent specimens of the local wild plants to the Provincial Museum at Victoria.

Time and time again he went to look at the pictographs. They were rare on the coast, he knew. Especially he liked the panel painting with its killer whales and its once-bright paint, now dimming under fungus and disintegrating under calcite seepage. Whatever fixative this artist had used—fish oil perhaps?—it had soaked into the rock, taking the paint with it. The substance would be there even when the form had gone.

Then there was an abstraction—of suns, perhaps?—which reminded him of a primitive he had seen in Africa. But he had met Thor Heyerdahl one day, when the latter came to look at and sketch the ancient art of the islands, and Heyerdahl had spoken about suns and South America. Solar discs, he said, with seven rays like this one could be found in Sweden, the Italian Alps, southern France, the Basque country, Portugal and Uzbekistan in Central Asia. Sun worship had been universal and its legends legion.

No wonder, thought John Pool, and especially in a climate like this. No wonder Indian chiefs had "smoked the sun" and the shamans put it into dance and story. Primitive culture mythology, nature: those were the subjects John had studied, by book and by observation ever since coming to Corydalis. They seemed to be in the very atmosphere of the place. Yet Elizabeth could not feel this at all. She had never liked it here. A pity. What a pretty girl she had been with her blue eyes and golden hair. She was a good-looking woman now. When she couldn't stand Corydalis—and him—any longer, she went to Vancouver to revel in hot baths and electric light and people. Who could blame her?

But more and more he wanted to stay home himself while Elizabeth took her trips or went to the Women's Institute meetings, whist nights, picnics, dances.

He thought a great deal as he worked on the cottage for his brother, who was coming to live on Cortes. It was above the bay by the brook, where there were broadleaf maples like huge suns in autumn. Five feet of boulders for the cottage walls, windows on three sides, a fireplace. The bottom boulders had been very big and Timmy was old now. He himself was slowing up, though he was only sixty-two. Elizabeth's hair was white as the cotton grass. But there had been these twenty protected—that word again!—and fruitful years. "I thank whatever gods there be!"

John patted the old horse and together, the stoneboat dragging behind them, they walked down the incline to the beach. He needed some big slabs of rock for doorsteps, but one was all Timmy could manage going up. It was a slow business now, he thought. Yet he liked doing it. Good to be out in the sun and he felt starved for fresh air somehow.

He struck his chest against a tightness in it and went on. At the cottage he stooped to roll the rock off the stoneboat. But when he tried to straighten up he went down instead, rolling sideways on the ground. There was no pain, only a great weariness and the air seemed to have thickened. How quickly it was getting dark. He hadn't realized it was so late. Perhaps the horse was blocking out the light. "Timmy," he whispered, "Timmy. . . . "

Because I felt myself a custodian, I felt that everything built by the Pools must be restored quickly, except the chicken house on the beach, where mink were now too prevalent. So everything has been renewed, even the bench in the woods where John and Elizabeth sat and looked out to sea, though now the trees at the water's edge are so tall that no sea can be seen. On the trails, in the forest, nothing has been changed—except for the logging-off, which began in the 1880s—and much has returned to what it was. If the old dwellers in these parts came back they would not lose their way.

I have added little. A new name, Channel Rock, as no corydalis grows wild here now and more farm-land, more flower beds, grass for a tiny patio and backyard, insulation in the attic, larger windows, a water pump, a small fibreglass boat with a four-horse-power outboard motor, shingle stain on the outside of the house and light paint inside. But the cat holes which John Pool cut so carefully in each and every outside door have all been boarded up. Our doors have better locks now and we don't leave tools lying around any more.

I feel that I am working here not only for myself, but for all those who were here before me. Although many people want to buy plants grown from those put in before my time, I never take money for them. They have been passed on to me, so I must pass them on in turn.

But not the one flower which comes up each year, sometimes in places where there is no bed at all. Always a different flower and always strange to me, because I did not plant it. A lily I never knew existed, the Rose of Sharon, hollyhocks and other plants which English oldtimers have identified for me. A bulb has finally risen to the surface again or a bulblet ripened underground. Soil has been disturbed and seeds dug up. That must be it.

At one time an amateur archaeologist came, looking for petroglyphs and pictographs. By boat and on foot he covered large stretches of Cortes and Marina Islands. Near Manson's Landing a fish nine feet long, buoyant and balanced on the high tide line mark, has been found on a beach boulder just north of the old Indian village of Paukeanum. He felt that this might have been done some two thousand years ago by an advanced artist: one of the Athapascan people who came from the interior on the first migration to the coast by way of the great rivers. "Even the myth of who did these carvings and why has passed out of the mind of man" he said. Perhaps the first wave of Athapascans came to Butler Point out of the Homathco River from Chilco Lake, then spread a little outwards into Johnstone Strait and north and south from there.

The head of the fish points towards The Gorge (called *Saiithl*—"Salt Lake,"—by the present Salish) where there are pictographs. Of one painting I saw—poorly placed and perhaps done by a novice—nothing remains but daubs of ochre. The fixative entered into the porous rock and drew the paint pigment with it, making it part of the rock. So the fading does not come from time and sunblaze, as many people think, but from slow erosion of the rock face itself, such as internal cracking and splitting, or calcite seep.

There is a panel which must have been magnificent before calcite seepage from a fairly recent internal rock cleavage eroded it. There is also an abstract figure, dimmed by fungus, containing what seems to be two suns separated by lines. A cavern recess, which mink inhabit now, shows ash and shellfish refuse not brought by animals. Also a smoke-blackened roof. Did shamans shelter here at one time ? Were the pictographers the ones vaguely referred to by the Kwakiutl as "the people of the Spirits?" The pictographing still goes on—or did. In 1950, near Seymour Inlet, I saw an Indian painting on a cliff face: an abstract of rays and angles.

It seems that the Gorge paintings might be around four hundred years old and done by the second coast-wave of Athapaskans, also plateau people, also of Salish origin. The Salish people living on Cortes Island now say they know nothing about them. But one, at least, felt that in the whole area there was "very high, very pure spirit, very strong." To the archaeologist and his son there was an air of "great mystery and omnipotence." It might have been part of a religious centre, the older man said; a place "deliberately chosen by the shamans. Here magic lived and had a real being once upon a time."

Now it is I who stand on this channel rock where so many people may have stood before me. Seven harlequins are swimming nearby and a big loon beyond them. Half a dozen herons fly home and a gull slants over a log where cormorants are preening. Two killer whales gambol through Uganda Passage and past Marina Island, perhaps truants trying to rejoin the pod which passed yesterday. A few weeks ago a duplicate of the big grizzled seal which used to follow my boat in early years turned up and now I can see him in Chetlo Bay.

Little in this scene can have changed through the centuries. Most of the changes have come since I did. The last big logging of virgin timber, the sulphurous cloud over Campbell River, lights on Quadra Island where there was only forest darkness, my weather station. Now too there are a scheduled airline service, an automatic blinker light and buoyed channel, the *Cortes Queen* ferrying over the strait, and the sound of many cars carried on the wind. In the summer thousands of tourists come with their planes, speedboats and opulent cruisers. But the spirit of the place has not changed and its springs of happiness have not dried up.[7]

As Gilean Douglas aged, the burden of physical work on a property with no electricity or roads and a large garden to maintain, as well as the lack of money, put her life on the island in jeopardy. Money would continue to be a problem, but the need for practical physical help was answered in 1959 with the arrival on the island of David Edwards. As a young man of 24, he had left Vancouver for adventure and began working on the *Columbia*. When the ship stopped on Cortes, he decided to stay on the island and found work doing odd jobs. His need for employment and a place to live coincided with Douglas's need for help. What began as a temporary situation became more permanent when he moved to her property to become resident caretaker and helper, living in the little building Douglas had thought to use as a writing studio. Their mutual dependency and responsibility was to continue for the next thirty-four years, with Edwards assuming more and more of the work as time went on.

Although the physical difficulties of staying at Channel Rock were eased, Douglas's financial position continued to worsen. Aside from her writing, her only income came from selling her garden produce and plants and from the few dividends still trickling in from the estate of her father. Her land was a substantial asset—her only one—but it was difficult to raise any money from it without destroying it. Although she sold some timber, extensive logging was out of the question. She was unwilling to take out a mortgage for fear that her worsening financial situation would prevent her from making the payments, and afraid to sell off part of the property lest it be further subdivided. An attempt to raise money by selling off all but ten acres failed when, just in time, she discovered that the buyer intended to divide the property into small lots. With the help of friends, the sale was narrowly averted.

When Douglas stepped down from her administrative role for the WI in 1960, she resolved to lessen her public commitments in order to have more time for her writing. To relieve her financial situation, she decided to pursue the interest that the Canadian Writers' Foundation had expressed in her work. In a series of letters, the Foundation requested information from her regarding her circumstances. She detailed the hardship of her life, which she summarized as follows: "I am now in the position of having to work such long hours to support myself and pay someone to do the hard physical work I can no longer manage (no electricity or other mod. cons. at Channel Rock!), such as cutting wood and digging over vegetables, that I have not been able to finish the work I care most about: these books."[8] After a further exchange of letters, the Foundation notified her in December of 1963 that "the Board has authorized a grant of $50.00 per month for January and February 1964: and if this amount is not sufficient for your needs kindly advise me and further consideration will be given to your grant."[9] This small but vitally important grant continued until the end of her life, gradually increasing to about two hundred dollars per month. It relieved some of the financial pressure and allowed Douglas to concentrate more on the writing she wished to do.

THE POET DEFIES

I am making beauty here
While the neighbours plot and plan;
While they whisper, "It is queer!
Find out everything you can.
Why the lamps burn through the night,
Why there is no stir by day;
Why the garden is a blight
And the steps are grimed and grey."

I am making beauty here—
Loveliness of leaf and sky
And of water lithe and clear
So it will not ever die.
Let the dust and litter blow!
Let the world be set and sane!
I can make a dead joy glow,
I can draw the sting of pain.[10]

Douglas had always placed her journalism in many venues, but now research for non-fiction articles of a general nature became more and more difficult because of her isolation and her financial problems. Her writing therefore began to centre increasingly on her life at Channel Rock and on philosophical ruminations about the seasons of nature and the cycles of life. She had been a feature writer for the *Victoria Daily Colonist* and the *Vancouver Sun* since the late 1940s and in 1961 her work for the *Daily Colonist* became a regular column, "Nature Rambles." This feature continued after the paper became the *Times Colonist* in 1980, and she would publish the monthly column until 1992—a crucial, steady source of income. Some of her finest writing appeared in these essays, later reworked for her book *The Protected Place*.

She continued to write poetry as well as nature articles, and two more books of poetry appeared: *The Pattern Set* (1958) and *Seascape with Figures* (1967). Between the help of Edwards and the myriad ways of making a living, Douglas managed to stay on the island and maintain her way of life. Her residence on the island now seemed relatively secure, but around her, island life was changing. With the imminent arrival of the ferry service and Hydro, the isolation of the island would be eased. Yet the very hardships of her life were also what made it precious, and Douglas looked on "progress" as a mixed blessing. She had become involved in the local ratepayers organization that was formed in 1963, and when the regional district of Comox-Strathcona was established in 1965, she was there to work for the creation of land use and zoning regulations.

Channel Rock
Christmas 1969

Dear Friends:

I have never seen a more glorious crescendo of the year than we had this October. The whole world seemed filled with golden light and all the forest trails were illuminated like old manuscripts. Mosaics of gold and rust were underfoot and the beaches of our small bays strewn with treasure. Oh, those bays! Each one a gift of glory and a reason for thanksgiving. Everywhere I went, everywhere I looked, were scenes so beautiful they hurt. This is too much, too much, I kept saying to myself. The earth is just too beautiful.

Too beautiful to keep, perhaps. At least it seems so when one thinks of the noise and smog and litter with which we are killing it and ourselves. During the past year I—as a member of the Comox-Strathcona Regional Board, the Cortes Planning Commission (there are 8 of us) and our Ratepayers executive—have been dealing with these matters. In two weeks, when the ferry starts running here, those problems and others will be on us. I feel myself that the beauty of our island is its greatest asset, but there are always those who can feel nothing but money in the pocket. We have them everywhere, and everywhere they are sacrificing the future to the present.

You can guess from the above that my year has been a busy and frustrating, but always interesting, one. As I am also Whaletown School Representative, secretary-treasurer of A.C.W. and a member of the Church Committee, the time so desperately needed for my own work has had to be stolen from sleep and even meals. Sometimes you wonder if it's worth it when you see people with nothing to do who want to do nothing. But of course that isn't the right way to look at things and I don't, except in moments of desperate tiredness. I must help where I can, no matter what others do or don't do. But—can we have peace—can we even survive—on apathy?

Last winter the landscape was as full of silver light as October was of gold. We had snow and snow and I just loved it. The sun shone, the air was so dry and the world so full of paw prints and winter wings. As all meetings were cancelled for January and February partly owing to a slide on the main road—I had hopes of catching up with myself. But when activities resumed in March I was still running at top speed—and losing ground all the time.

In March I gave the talk on the World Day of Prayer and managed to spend a few days with each of two friends on the island, because of meetings in their communities. Also I got my telephone; the first I've had in 20 years. I'm of two minds whether it's a blessing or a curse, but at least I don't have to walk or boat six miles now to send a message.

In March and April—planting and meetings—and church, of course—came before dances and parties. At the end of April I flew to Vancouver (the bus strike was on) for a glorious three weeks of visiting friends there and elsewhere. I could write reams about those happy days! Also about the audiences when I spoke in halls and colleges about the work of Regional District boards.

It was a good thing I had the change and rest—though part of the time was spent in research—as June crashed in with customers, visitors, fans, tourists, parties of all sorts—and always, always work and meeting. Towards the end of the month I went down to Vancouver again, this time on a purely research trip. I might say that in May the temperature went up to nearly 80 and in June to almost 90. The rainfall was under 2" for the two months combined. I'm just different or possibly I have snowbird blood. Heat and I don't get along.

July was more of the same in weather, but tripled in activities. Our annual Barbeque was a great success, with the yachts anchored six deep. After that, spare moments had to be gouged out of nowhere to get ready for the Fiesta in early August. It too had happy crowds and every last little thing was sold. The rest of the month was duplicate of July and I have never in my life known a summer to whiz by with such speed. I seemed to be making up the monthly weather report every week!

Most of the tourists vanished in September, but otherwise things didn't slacken very much. In October the local merry-go-round went faster, if possible, and here am I in November with the farm work only half done and the garden not tucked into bed. I have never been as far behind as this, even though I am up before daylight and it is usually midnight before I'm in bed. But you must give me credit for turning down the chairmanship of the Centennial Committee and that there are now two organizations in which I don't hold office any more!

There will be all sorts of doings when the ferry comes in: here, on Quadra Island and at Campbell River. In Whaletown we shall have ribbon-cutting and speeches, with 28 dignitaries and their wives from Victoria, Courtenay and C.R. A buffet luncheon at one of our halls will be followed by a cruise on the *Cortes Queen* for all those who can climb aboard (weather permitting!) and a dance in the evening.

Other changes will be the Hydro creeping steadily across the island and a relief map at the ferry landing showing our roads and points of interest. Our 1971 Centennial project is a hikers' trail over some of the loveliest parts of Cortes. We were the first community in B.C. to take on a project and also the first to go into regional district planning. We on the Planning Commission are working on land use zoning, fire protection, garbage disposal, trailer camps, parks and all the other problems coming with progress—which not always is. I still believe that if even one island on this coast could be left without a ferry and in its pristine state that the rush of would-be residents and tourists would be tremendous. With small farms and artisans, the economic problem could be solved and there would be some very happy people in that world. But—well, I won't go into the screams of protest from those with gold spots before the eyes!

I feel like celebrating this year myself. Not the coming of power and the ferry, but the 20 years I have had without them. What glorious years they have been!

My alarm clock in the morning—the big loon in the bay (one stays with me all year)—or the song of a robin on the hawthorn. The cry of a gull, the zylophone of an eagle, the shriek of a great blue heron announcing visitors on the trail— these were the constant music of my day. But loveliest of all, perhaps, was the singing of wind in the evergreens and the melody of water flowing. Always the sparkling air, the clear sea, the far mountains capped with snow. Always the big sky over my head dazzling with sun, glinting with stars, opal with cloud. An otter family playing in the bay, the perfume of laundry blowing on the line, a seal mother teaching her baby to swim and, except at tourist times, silence like the hand of God soothing and healing.

Bald eagles and great blue heron are on the endangered list now. All summer long litter fringes the beaches and the ubiquitous plastic container bobs on the waves. Tourists use the roadside and woods as dumping grounds for their waste. Between speed craft and planes, it is hard to make oneself heard at times. Boats like my little one are endangered by the swells of arrogant yachts hurrying through present beauty towards some future delight. Only to race through that also because it in turn has become the present. How mad we mortals be!

In my lifetime I have known mountain, desert, forest and seacoast in all their natural glory. I have lived in cities before they became cemeteries and in small communities before neighbourliness was sacrificed to supermarkets. I have travelled the roads of this continent before they were strangled by cars and worked on farms that had not yet become factories. So whatever happens now I shall have had not only these 20 years, but all the years before them. Is it any wonder that I consider myself one of the happiest and luckiest persons in the world?

This has been a long screed about myself and me, my and I. But I have sent letters to so few of you who have written me in 1969 that I felt you should know as much as possible of what I did and thought in the year almost gone. Though I have hardly mentioned writing—which has gone fairly well—or travel and holiday fun or many other things. My broken ankle and two bouts of flu I haven't mentioned at all or the sad times when friends passed on.

Forgive me for all my omissions and believe me when I say that though I speak of me, I think of you. Not business or beauty, anxiety or content, laughter or tears, can ever make me forget you. You are my dear friends, always.[11]

Although Douglas often looked back and wrote from memory, she was also a forward-looking person who could face the future—good or bad. And what she saw as a future possibility was the very destruction of the natural world, with its silence and solitude, that had enriched her life. Not one to rest on her laurels, she entered her seventieth year as a champion and often leader of the fight to preserve the island environment. Once more the Battle Maid took up the challenge.

CHAPTER 9

The World Catches Up

*F*or both Gilean Douglas and Cortes Island, 1970 marked a change. The arrival of a ferry service brought the increased pressure of more people and more desire for subdivision of the land. "Another thing which saddens me is the 'progress' of our beautiful island," she wrote in her 1971 Christmas letter.

> It was inevitable that with the coming of the ferry, there would be changes. But every tree that goes down to widen the roads (blacktopping has begun), every subdivision that starts up, every marina and supply depot (for Hydro and BC Tel) that opens, gives me a heart stab. Our island was so unspoiled, so private and free, so dear and familiar to us all. Now I can go into a crowded store and not know a single customer's face. I can walk the roads and not recognize one of the many cars that go by. Although I have lived here 22 years, sometimes I feel like a stranger now.[1]

These changes led Douglas to focus her community service work more and more on local politics, where she could help guide the future development of the island. The Regional District of Comox-Strathcona had been formed in 1965, with Cortes designated Electoral Area I. Under this form of government, rural electoral areas and municipalities within a region were represented on a board that handled many of the functions of local government such as land use, planning, zoning by-laws, waste management, pollution, and transportation.

Each rural electoral area had an elected Director and Alternate Director, and an Advisory Planning Commission. The Cortes APC was the only one in the province which was elected by and from the Ratepayers rather than appointed by the Director. Although Area I had a population of fewer than five hundred and was the smallest in the province, it had been the first to undertake a comprehensive, long-term planning process. When the population began to grow, zoning regulations for the control of land use were already in place.

Douglas had been elected Alternate Director for Area I in 1968. In 1973 she took over as Director, a position she held until 1978. She was interested in the political process and in planning. She deplored the crisis-approach style of development and supported the creation of an Official Settlement Plan to regulate development on the island. Under her guidance, the island's Settlement Plan became the first one completed in the Regional District. On the Environment Committee, she addressed such issues as preservation of wetlands and salmon habitat enhancement—long before environmental concerns were widely recognized and supported.

In her fostering of participation in the local political process, as in her concern for planning, she was on the cutting edge of governance on the islands. From her position as a representative on the Regional Board, Douglas kept an eagle eye on upcoming political issues, alert to the implications for Cortes. She felt strongly that everybody living on the island had a duty to be involved in the decision-making process, and she encouraged public participation by circulating Director's Reports several times a year. She also did not hesitate to phone people and exhort them to attend important meetings. As she railed in one Director's Report, "If you don't like the way things are being done right here, say so, out loud; or get elected to office and try to change them. Don't believe that old canard about one person being helpless to change anything. All the changes of this world began with just one person."[2]

Central to Douglas's philosophy of development was the need to balance the human and the natural worlds. "There are moments when I wonder if the way of the conservationist isn't harder than that of the transgressor," she wrote in "Good Lord Deliver Us."

So many transgressors seem to flourish and conservationists seldom do. Transgressors are either pitied or condemned; conservationists are both, and laughed at too. All that is needed to become the hilarious life of some non-nature meetings is to suggest conserving scenery or preserving wild life. At best such would-be saviours are patted on the head with tolerant words and dismissed like children, imbeciles or lacy valentines. . . .

You will still hear people say that the best things in life are free. But some of the best things of our past life can't be had at all, any more. Whole species of birds and animals have been wiped out, whole stretches of lovely land laid waste. Soon the only beauty and wildness left will be in parks and zoos, where we shall have to pay to see them. . . .

Then there is man, an endangered species indeed, both physically and spiritually. Despite all the scientific proof of what crowding, noise and pollution do to our ears, eyes, lungs and nervous systems, we continue to slide down the apathy road to our destruction. Is our death wish then so strong? What hope for peace if we are so filled with acts of war, even against ourselves? We continue to *fight* nature, we set out to *conquer* the universe; we do not seem to know even the vocabulary of co-operation with either.[3]

Douglas took the sometimes unpopular position that land use and, by extension, population, had to be controlled, since unchecked growth would destroy the very environment that attracted people to the island. She was firm in opposing the pressure for unrestricted development. From her Summer 1977 Director's Report:

"You islanders!" a woman screamed at me during a seminar, when I had been speaking about limiting island population. "Who do you think you are? Everyone should be able to live on your island." Carry that to its logical conclusion and you would sink poor old Cortes.

Nevertheless there are too many people set on destroying the islands with too many people. Not that they think of themselves as destroyers. On the contrary. "We must share with others," they insist earnestly. "Just because we were here first we can't be selfish. The islands are so beautiful!"

So by-laws are changed to cut the limited land into smaller and smaller pieces. More ferries and roads are needed to handle the increased population. These bring in more people again and the cycle is repeated. Danger from fire grows and a fire district is established. As trees go down to clear the land for homes, the water table does too. Deeper wells are a must, at higher and higher prices. Watersheds are in danger. Water districts are created, sewers are installed, garbage dumps enlarged. With each such improvement taxes rise. Older residents are forced to sell, younger residents clamor for jobs. Industry comes in and the last of beauty and seclusion go out. The very things which brought people to the islands in the first place have been destroyed.

The Greeks had a motto: *Auden Agen,* "Nothing Too Much." Let us ponder it.[4]

Douglas's strength as a planner was her ability to envision the future consequences of present action. "The great thing is to have imagination; to project on the screen of our minds not only today but tomorrow. Short-term dreams of convenience can turn into long-term nightmares. Small improvements are like pussycats; they grow bigger. Residents have said to me: 'I didn't think about the ferry bringing people here; I only thought about getting outside myself.' So let us examine each suggested step of progress with microscopic eyes. What will this mean 5, 10, 20 years from now? Do I want this island to be like so many other crowded, noisy places or do I want it to be a place where residents and visitors can find beauty, quiet, a sense of stability and that feeling of difference in life style that can be so stimulating and enjoyable. I haven't noticed all that much happiness in the places where gadgets grow."[5]

Douglas found allies for her position in a group of newcomers, the "back to the land" arrivals who also eschewed the reliance on technology and sought an alternative to the urban world. "New neighbours are all around me: young couples—'long hairs and granny gowns'—as some describe them. I like these young people very much and many of the things they believe, I believe also. As I tell them, I am so glad that at last the world is catching up with me! What they are practising of simple, green-earth living, organic eating and peaceful, friendly ways, I have believed in all my life."[6]

Not only did these new residents become political allies, they were also friends. With her zest for new experiences, Gilean enjoyed getting to know the young people, who recognized her as a fellow spirit and wise elder.

In June also we—all young people except myself—held our Midsummer Madness. Fun! It began with an ancient incantation and ended with a bonfire, fireworks, guitars and bongo drums. In between we bound a wheel with paper and sparkler, set it afire and rolled it down the cliff beside my house. Perhaps you don't know that if the wheel stays upright and ends in the water, as ours did, crops will be good. We were all growers, so we took three charred sticks from the fire and planted them as a triangle in our vegetable fields to make crops better.

A handful of ashes from the fire, placed on my roof, was to make sure that the house did not burn down in the next year. There was a lot of laughter and the food—all organic, including my strawberries—was delicious.[7]

Almost every year of the seventies was characterized in the annual Christmas letter as the "busiest year ever," and no wonder. Now in her seventies (though her age was a closely guarded secret), Douglas had a tremendous vitality and many active interests. She attended Regional Board meetings, worked on two books and a monthly newspaper column, maintained a large and beautiful garden from which she sold plants and produce, kept up a voluminous correspondence, entertained legions of visitors, and travelled for work and pleasure. She inhabited an aging body, but was youthful in her appreciation for new ideas and willingness to take on new challenges.

Still, much as Douglas enjoyed the stimulation of new places and new people, she always returned to Channel Rock with a sense of joy and relief.

Home. The brown and pink house nestled at the foot of the tall cliff and taller trees. The big loon in the bay, harlequins on the rocks, scoters scooting along the water just for fun. When I have to leave all this for a time and am flying back again, I look down at the little house and say: "There it is!"

"Didn't you expect it to be?" teases the pilot. Yes, I did, but I just have to make myself believe all over again that it's true. It is a pleasure to stay with friends "outside," but coming home is a special thing because of the many years when I was homeless.[8]

Gilean Douglas had sought long and hard, far and wide, for a sense of home. She was granted her heart's desire in her mountain cabin, but when she was driven from that paradise, she again wandered and sought a place in nature. Her Cortes Island home became her new haven, but only after a struggle. Finally, in the "Protected Place," she recaptured the sense of belonging and safety that she had experienced as a child. Here, as in the mountains, she found the freedom and the inspiration for her work.

The seventies were a decade of harvest in Douglas's writing life. "Nature Rambles" continued to appear regularly in the *Daily Colonist*. A collection of poetry, *Now in This Night*, was published in 1973. The manuscript of her life in the mountains, which had been written in the forties, was finally accepted for publication in 1978 as *Silence Is My*

Homeland—by Gilean Douglas. This work, more than the previously published collection, *River for My Sidewalk*, recorded the period of her life in the mountains and expressed the solace, silence, and sense of homecoming that were part of her experience there. The *Silence* manuscript won first prize in the 1978 National Writers' Club competition, a prize offered to the best unpublished manuscript submitted during the year. Because of the exceptional strength of the work, the National Writers' Club took the unprecedented step of assisting with the book's publication. Long rejected by a string of publishers, the final acceptance of the manuscript (and of the gender of its author) was another indication that the world was catching up with Douglas. In addition, when *River for My Sidewalk* was revised and reissued in 1984, it too went out under her own name. As Douglas later told a *Vancouver Sun* reporter, she had "killed off" Grant Madison because it was no longer impossible to imagine that a woman had lived the life described in the mountain books.[9]

With *Silence Is My Homeland*, Douglas's love and longing for the mountains went out to her community of readers. The following year, *The Protected Place* appeared in print, balancing her love of the mountains with that of the sea. Channel Rock was now truly her home.

This July dawn burst so suddenly over the mainland mountains that you could almost hear the bang. Multihued confetti of cloud drifted across the sky. It was like a wedding where the guests were given white paper bags of coloured confetti to blow up and break over the bride and groom.

Sometimes, on a morning like this, I sing. Very badly, but I doubt if that matters when there's no human to hear you. I sing to the pearling sky and the dove-feathered sea and the light unfolding like another, sweeter song. Because the papoose wind of dawn has bird chirps on its breath. Because this new day has come into my arms for a moment, like a child just wakened from sleep. Because the sea has begun to chatter to the shore and I like what it's saying.

The very air is diamant. The sands run golden away on this low tide down to an ocean alive with morning. Life shoots up from the earth in grass and flowers and trees. It is the same fountain of life which is in all things visible and invisible.

The sea has begun to sing sweetly of morning. Her song follows me up the trail to the barn. Her song has followed me all my life, among all my wanderings in the mountains and the sage. I think of her by the well and in the rain and beside my small silver seam of a brook which stitches the greens of this July together. . . .

*David Edwards soon after
he arrived on Cortes in 1959.*

The studio at Channel Rock that became Edwards' home.

Douglas (centre) with friends, 1959.

*Douglas (left) en route to
a meeting, c. 1965.*

Douglas, 1972.

The Cortes Queen *at Heriot Bay, Quadra Island, on her inaugural run in 1970.*

"New neighbours are all around me: young couples—'long hairs and granny gowns'—as some describe them. I like these young people very much. . . ."

Douglas with friend and neighbour Peggy Norris, 1970.

Douglas and one of many visitors, 1972.

Peggy Norris and Arn Saba, 1971.

Douglas on Christmas morning, 1975.

At home at Channel Rock, late 1970s.

The rock in front of Douglas's cabin was bright with bulbs, heather, and flowers planted in beds made in crevices.

The daffodils Douglas planted on the little tidal island in front of her home still bloom every spring.

196

But sometimes it's almost more than I can do in July to keep up with all that's going on at Channel Rock. Visitors, though many, are the least of it. The worms have hatched one brood and are contemplating another. Bees and hummingbirds work assembly lines all day, while hawk moths take the night shift. Soil dwellers keep going round the clock and near the root-house that wraith plant, Indian pipe, seems like one of them as it allies itself with fungus and feeds on rotting wood. Red admiral butterflies are feeding on stinging nettles. Caterpillars are munching their own particular delicacies. Beetles are boring, birds are hunting, pollen is flying, mosquitoes are biting, herons are fishing, otters are sliding, ducks are ducking, crickets are fiddling, mink are swimming, wasps are annoying. All the fruits and vegetables seem to be ripening at once and if one more deer eats one more rose I shall scream.[10]

Gilean Douglas always shared a special bond with animals. In the wild, they provided focal points for some of her most inspired nature writing; at home, they provided unconditional companionship. Inevitably, these creatures also became subjects of her writing. One of her most beloved pets was Black Frosty, a cat who shared Gilean's home and life at Channel Rock and founded a royal line.

MY BLACK FROSTY

Two years after I came to Channel Rock I heard a sound at the back door and opened it to find a starving, half-wild cat outside. On our community bulletin board I put up a sign: "FOUND one small black cat, large yellow eyes, white mark on upper chest." The owner called and finding Carbon (as I named her later) purring on my lap, suggested that I keep her. They had her half-grown kitten, he said, and apparently one house was too small for two feminine felines. The mother had run away weeks before.

So Carbon was my first cat ever. Copy, a small replica of herself, was her first kitten. Her last kitten was an only child and too soon an orphan. This tiny black mite with the white splotch on its chest was my charge, to be fed with an eye-dropper and greatly loved. Remembering the weather and the chill that had come into my own life at that time, I named her—perhaps unkindly—Black Frost: Frosty for short.

I am not sure what might have happened to me in those dark days if she had not been there: a dependent mite to be fed, kept warm, housebroken and even taught how to manicure her claws on a tree. When I typed she lay just where the carriage of the machine wouldn't touch her in its swing. When I worked on the land she spent day after day scampering up and down the vegetable rows or dropping suddenly into a patch of shade, to sleep.

When I took the trail to town she went into my packsack, out of which her pert black head with its tip-tilted nose would peek with friendly impertinence. Left at home when she became too big to carry with the rest of my load, she would meet me a mile down the trail. She learned that other, larger cats and even dogs lurked on the rest of the way to town, which was gravelled road. But when her kittens were given to neighbours she braved even those dangers to go to them. . . .

Certainly Frosty recognized the tones of my voice—and how she loved to pretend she didn't when I wanted her to do something distasteful. But I learned a few things too. When I saw her big topaz eyes looking at me sideways I knew that she was up to no good. Bedtime was the time to lick a little cat food, sip a little milk, sip and sup, sup and sip, until I rose in my wrath and pushed her out the door.

If a meal was delayed I would find a mouse lying reproachfully on the doorstep. Exasperated one evening that I should forget her bedtime snack just because I had guests, she chased a mouse into the living room. The party got livelier by the moment and certainly a mouse was chased out while the cat was kept in. But at three A.M. I discovered a mouse—the same? another?—in the bookcase.

Determined that her current pussy should have enough protein, Frosty one night brought in a squirrel which promptly got away and went to chatter on top of a precious Chinese vase on a high shelf. Frosty jumped, so did the squirrel and my horrified eyes saw the vase toppling forward. So I jumped also, but too late. The vase fell—unbroken—into the paper-filled box where a kitten crouched in terror. That was only a week before Frosty brought in the ferret. Fed to the teeth with wild life, I blocked up all the cat doors cut by my predecessors, except the one in the attic.

This only encouraged the mighty hunter to take on bigger game. That Hallowe'en I looked out the window, in the light of a waning moon, to see Frosty and a stranger cat flying up the trail after a coon. Having been told that coons are death on cats, I flew up the trail too. (Nothing like animals to keep you in good condition!) The stranger cat disappeared, the coon made for the stream at the side of the orchard. When he reached it Frosty slowed down, stopped, and then nonchalantly sniffed some grass as though that had been the only reason for her marathon. Evidently she knew all about the ways of a coon with a cat in water.

Not that water by itself bothered Frosty. She thought nothing of rain and one of her favourite outdoor sports used to be catching crabs in the sea shallows. She would also go after clams with her paws, digging holes like a dog. When I went swimming she would pick her way daintily to the farthest rock not under water and stand there until I came out, even though the tide was coming in. In a boat her dignity was appalling. She preferred the bow seat and from it she viewed the world and me like an over-seer of galley slaves. When I used the outboard only a very brisk breeze could shatter her royal poise.

One night I was wakened from a deep sleep by what I thought was a scream. I found myself in the middle of the living room floor, without knowing how I got there, just as the sound was repeated. This time I recognized a mink's screech and the sound my usually silent, partly Persian Frosty made when roused to fury. She and her two babies had been sleeping on the mat outside the back door, but only one kitten was there now. I found the other, a paw bent ominously, about forty feet away. Not knowing whether mink or cat would win a battle, I left the baby to follow the caterwauling towards the beach. The sounds were hideous and always just ahead of me. Then there was a sudden, complete silence.

Dreading what I might find, I played my flashlight along the shore to where a pair of eyes shone green in the darkness. Frosty was behind the eyes, alone. She wasn't exactly spitting on her paws and yowling: "Bring on your mink!" but I felt she might at any moment. Of the mink there was no sign, but the next day it passed the house as usual. Only this time Frosty got to her feet and the mink, swerving abruptly, took to the ocean. I didn't see it again. The "green stick" break of the pussy healed perfectly.

There are many black and white photographs in my memory album. Frosty carrying her two quite heavy kittens down from the attic to drop them and herself on my chest in the middle of the night, when she discovered that I had turned the house over to guests and gone to sleep in the barn. Frosty streaking up a tree, but with a backward look to catch my expression of amazement and praise: "What a wonderful pussy!" Frosty climbing trees, rocks and woodpiles so she could jump down on my back. But once she walked out on a branch that would hardly hold her weight, to step quietly and softly to my shoulder when she sensed that I needed comforting.

When she needed help herself—at a miscarriage, when her babies were coming, when a kitten was hurt—there would be the same softly urgent sound repeated until she was sure I understood. Once I didn't and she grabbed the bottom of my slacks to pull me the way I should go. I learned her mouse cry early—and promptly saw that all doors were shut. She never asked aloud for food, but when she thought her very small tidbit of liver had been forgotten she jumped up on a certain kitchen chair and looked unutterable things. When I answered her taps on the French door and let her in or out, she came and went without a sound. But if it was night and she had wakened me, there was a little soft murmur as she passed, like a thank you. Winter nights were never so long when she lay on my lap as I read and across my feet when I slept. Of course the morning would find her black head on the pillow beside me. Sometimes I sang her a lullaby:

> I love my dear Frosty,
> I love her so much;
> I love her black fur
> that is soft to the touch;
> I love her gold eyes
> and her tip-tilted nose—
> I love her, I love her
> wherever she goes.

Frosty didn't suffer fools gladly and that applied to her children and grandchildren as well as to humans. Dogs she didn't suffer at all. Friends arriving with their setter were afraid he might hurt Frosty. They needn't have worried. Hearing her war cry, I looked out to see the setter running up the trail with ears back and tail down. He didn't even return for supper and his owners found him waiting for them at the civilized road, halfway home. Dogs or humans, all of them have had to bear Frosty's dignified look of appraisal and judgment. Nor did she ever become a sweet little old lady. She was a matriarch of dignity and character. It used to feel like an accolade then when she took my wrist gently in her mouth to tell me she loved me. As her glossy, long, black fur became a dull, dark brown and her whiskers silver, Frosty meant more to me than ever. I think she knew it.

I suppose I saved Frosty's life when her mother died. I have an idea she saved mine. One alone November there were three weeks of constant storms, when no boats passed the house and only windfalls came on my trail. That was when I came down with 'flu which turned into pneumonia. My temperature soared and finally I didn't want to eat or even to get up any more. But there was Frosty. I couldn't let her starve, I must let her out and in, I must keep the house warm. So when I put down some cat food for her, I made something to eat for myself. When I dragged myself up to let her out, I got wood for the fire. These were things which had to be done for something alive, even if I didn't care if I died myself. Die? Perhaps when Frosty was inside and might starve if no one came for weeks? It was unthinkable. So by the time the weather bettered I too was on the mend.

Although I had to be away quite often on business, I had kind neighbours and I never doubted that my well-fed cat would come running to meet me as I swung down the trail towards home. Then one summer a friend stayed in my house while I was gone for three months. When I got back she told me that Frosty hadn't been seen since a week after I left. My heart plummeted and for the next two days Meg must have found me poor company indeed. On the third day she went back to her own home and I went up the trail to the barn, feeling the greatest urge to call Frosty. How silly that would be, after all these months! But I called just the same. And down the trail, trotting at first and then breaking into a gallop, came my dear old pussy cat. She looked bigger and better than ever, but where she had been and why I never did find out.

I was away again in November of the following year, when the temperature nose-dived to zero on Cortes Island. So did my heart when a letter came saying that Frosty had been missing for over two weeks. It was almost Christmas when I finally managed to get home and I wasn't looking forward to the holiday at all. Listlessly, I started to do some Christmas baking the morning after I got back. The weather had warmed up a bit and snow had fallen. It was a beautiful, clear day and I opened the kitchen door to look up the bluff behind the house which was now a dazzlement of sun. Then I thought I must have spots before the eyes. But surely that was something very black moving down the cliff? It was indeed. It was

Frosty. She looked magnificently healthy and her coat shone like jet in the sun. . . .

What delightful Decembers those were when Frosty and I went bark gathering for the special Christmas woodpile. Along the shore and then into the woods, Frosty racing up trees or running along a branch to drop down on my back. One gala day we saw a tall dead fir fall, showering thick bark as it came down.

When I took Christmas mail into the post office in my little boat, a sad Frosty stayed home. Once I remained longer than I had intended in our small community and faced a three-mile boat ride in sleet and darkness, with a three-horsepower motor. A south-easter was rising rapidly. I had a flashlight, but it was dimming and if I took time to borrow one the storm would be up in the channel and might prove more than my little boat could handle.

It almost did. When I started to go round the headland, where there are always cross seas, I could see well enough to know that I couldn't make it. I turned back and waited, while the darkness deepened. I had a heavy load of parcels, papers and groceries and I thought about putting them ashore, but decided against it. That would mean another trip and the weight did keep the boat's head down just enough so the wind couldn't swing her.

When a lull came, I tried for the point once more and got too far to turn back. The south-easter was roaring towards me up the channel, the waves running white in the darkness. All I could do was try to hold her steady and quartering into the seas, while praying the little outboard motor wouldn't stop. As in all periods of crisis, time telescoped and I have no idea how long it took me to run into the partial shelter of three uninhabited bays and then out again into the storm. The sleet was cutting into my face, the boat was sloshing with water and I was semi-paralysed with cold. The wind was rising in big gusts and it seemed that each wave must bring broadside and disaster.

Finally I ducked behind a tiny island and then came out into the open for the last time before heading for the runway to my beach. It was black as deep mourning and I couldn't see ahead far enough to steer for a mountain. My failing flashlight failed to show me much of anything. However, I kept it focussed on the shore and aimed where I thought the runway ought to be. Then I saw two small green lights to port and changed course to head for them. The green lights were Frosty's eyes and she was sitting in the middle of the runway.

When it was too stormy to go for the mail by sea in the Christmas season, I took to the woods with a parcel-filled dunnage bag over each shoulder. Then Frosty went with me as far as the road, to wait there well hidden from the community dogs. Six laden miles it was altogether, but it seemed like almost nothing. So light of heart we were, so filled with the season's sorcery.

It was in December that Frosty left me, lighthearted and loving to the last in spite of her years. Now in this December, I can see her still: chasing the Santa Claus wrappings around the room, playing tug of war with me and a ribbon. She enchants my memories as she did my days.

Shortly after Frosty died I was just falling asleep one night when I felt the side of my bed move, the way it does when a cat jumps on it. There was the usual weight against my left leg and, again as usual, I put down my hand sleepily to stroke silky fur. My hand touched nothing. There was nothing there.

This has been repeated at intervals and sometimes I wake up in the night feeling something warm against me, between the blanket and the comforter. But when I look for the dark head that should be on my pillow, there is nothing.

It is ten years since Frosty died and only at quite long intervals now do I have this feeling of her presence. Rubbing against my ankle as I work among the vegetables, sitting on the chair arm beside me, jumping up in my lap. I am not thinking of her at these times. I am not grieving for her. Her daughter, Frosty Too, and I are happy together.

"Does Frosty Too react to any of this?" I have been asked. So far she hasn't been around or I haven't noticed. But two or three times I have thought she was walking in front or beside me, only to find her across the room staring at a spot near me with a strange, startled look.

I would like to believe, as some people do, that Frosty comes back to Channel Rock where she was loved so much. But the hard-headed, practical side of me raises a question mark. Let us say I have an open mind. Let us say I hope I am still living in this world when the answer comes: when the scientists discover laws of nature we have only dreamed about till now.[11]

As the 1970s drew to a close, Douglas's thoughts turned to the end of the year and the end of her life. She was approaching eighty and, while filled with plans and projects, she had to consider carefully how she would spend her remaining time. In 1977, she decided not to run for another term as Regional Director, and stepped down when her term ended in December. There was so much writing left to do, and even in the name of public service, she could no longer deny the pen.

CHAPTER 10

An October Moon

*G*etting older is just the nuisance of the world," Gilean Douglas wrote in one of her Christmas letters.[1] As she entered her eighties, she had to come to terms with the fact that her body couldn't be pushed as hard as it could be even a decade before. Nevertheless, her energy level remained high. She steadfastly refused to let anyone know her age, not wanting to be judged unfairly on that basis.

Douglas comments on aging in her essay "The Years Have Surprised Me," written in 1980. Some writers, she says,

referred to older people as though they became half wits or regressed to childhood the day after retirement. They infuriated me.

Others calmed me down. I rejoiced in those of eighty-odd who told me they felt a quarter, a third or half their age. Full of youth and strength and daring inside themselves. More power to them! In fact, I almost began to think that most people under ninety-nine—the age of a former school teacher of mine who still tosses a French phrase my way to see if I can still field it—were not old, but merely aging; as are we all. But in our zany manner we actually take credit for being young. "Man, the most intelligent of the animals—and the most silly," declared Diogenes.

"Her organs were like those of a young girl," said a doctor after doing an autopsy on a woman of sixty-eight killed in an accident. Quite so. We use the artificial reckoning of years, but nature uses the true reckoning of spirit. A woman or man of eighty by our time may be half that by nature's clock. By our reckoning Frosty Too, my cat, is ninety-eight years old and so flighty you wouldn't believe. Yet there is no tapping of foreheads as is seen too often when elderly humans do the dancing.

Florida Scott-Maxwell writes in *The Measure of My Days*: "My seventies were interesting and fairly serene, but my eighties are passionate. I grow more intense as I age. To my own surprise I burst out with hot conviction . . . though drab outside—wreckage to the eye—we flame inside with a wild life that is almost incommunicable."[2]

Throughout the eighties, Gilean's health problems worsened. Almost every year she suffered a debilitating bout of flu, and her goitre was acting up again, swelling and exerting pressure on her windpipe. Even worse, she had several small heart attacks and was diagnosed with congestive heart failure. Her heart problems were related to the strain of a lifelong struggle with a malfunctioning thyroid—a struggle that became more difficult in her advancing years, when she no longer had the same resilience or stamina.

But again she refused the doctor's advice for an operation on her goitre. Continuing her research into her various medical problems, she would pick and choose among the remedies suggested by her physicians, usually favouring herbal medicines and willpower. "The spirit speaks and the body believes," she wrote in 1984, and since she had an indomitable will, her eighties continued as a productive time.[3]

I HAVE LIVED WITH THESE

I do not know that I shall kiss again
the lips of summer or the brow of spring
or touch the hand of golden autumn when
she sits enraptured of remembering.

So now there is no dawn I do not see,
no day in which I do not find delight
and I sit, speechless, when in ecstasy
the moon pours out her passion on the night.

Let death come down in darkness and in pain—
I shall not fear it! I have lived with these
and my small dust will find the tender rain
and lie in rest below the singing trees.[4]

Still, Douglas's life became more circumscribed due to diminishing finances and failing health. She travelled less, and sought no public offices or other community duties. Yet Channel Rock and Gilean Douglas continued to fascinate and attract, and she was not isolated. Many who knew her, particularly those of younger generations, found in Gilean a model and mentor. Frequent visitors spent time with her, and her faithful island friends helped in any way they could so that she could remain at Channel Rock.

Most faithful was David Edwards. Over the years, Gilean and David had established strong bonds of trust and friendship, and David felt it his duty to assume more and more of the responsibility for daily life at Channel Rock as Gilean's health declined. Gardener, woodsman, cook, homemaker, and nurse, Edwards also became unofficial social secretary and tour guide. The path to Douglas's door was so trodden that she had to ration guests to one or two afternoons a week to allow time for her writing, and Edwards served as gatekeeper as well.

Ironically, poor health imposed the conditions of quiet and solitude that writing demanded and that Douglas had always sought. Time was short and the desire to complete her life's work was pressing. Questions of identity began to preoccupy her as she wrote steadily in her carefully protected morning hours. In the essay "Who Am I?", an article she revised for a sequel to *The Protected Place*, she explored her identity as a poet.

In my mad moments I dare to call myself a poet. I feel that word like a pain and a joy. Inspiration springs up inside me like a fountain of truth and light. For a little while—a few moments, an hour, half a day—I am flooded and illuminated by it. My thoughts and words run like sunlit water. I hug myself with happiness.

Then gradually my thoughts slow and the light begins to fade. I am tired and cannot see clearly any more. Soon my words walk instead of run and my thoughts flicker out into the dull of everyday. I have wakened from my dream.

For all poets, for all dreamers, let me beg this: let us wake naturally. Leave us alone when we hang "Do Not Disturb" on the door of our being. Do not knock or call or even whisper "I love you." If you truly love, you will protect the dreamer, even from yourself and even if you cannot understand him or his dream. This is magic and myth and saviour and you ignore it at your peril.

The scientists have proved that we must dream if our sleep is to be healthy. Perhaps the world is sick because so many in it have never dreamed or dream no longer. Perhaps dreams are fewer because people and things are many. A poet needs a quiet space where his dreams can run like happy children with no time clock to call them in to everyday.

We will tire in all too short a while, but for that while please do not fret or drop bricks or ask us to write you letters for your loneliness. Don't you understand? We are trying to make magic for you, such magic that when you read or hear or see it in a gallery you will know that you have come to your true home and can never be lonely again. A letter may fill the need of one person; a poem may fill the needs of thousands.

But if you intrude, if the spell is broken, then come anger, frustration, and such a feeling of bitter loss that, for a moment, the dreamer could kill those who are killing his true self, trampling his fragile magic. The weaker among us may let themselves be called or cajoled or herded along, leaving only an echo where their dreams used to be. This world is full of rage and frustration and echoes of dreams.

If you love us—especially if you love us—let us go away when we must, to weave our own spells of love for you and for us all. Never fear, we shall come back to you. If you let us return in our own time we shall come back revitalized, refreshed, all our emptiness filled with laughter. There may be a strangeness at first—after all we have been in fairyland, in our own private heaven—but soon our eyes will refocus, our hands be warm in your own again.

Perhaps what the poet needs is a desert, which has almost the last space and silence and solitude; which has an April in every raindrop.

It has been said that "even spring has no delight in a strange land." But what land is strange?

Everywhere I have been there were the familiar faces of birds and flowers, animals and people. The language might be strange, but what of that? There is always the language of the heart, which is the same in all countries. "A joyful heart filled with love is everywhere at home."

Particularly with those termed eccentric by the unseeing. The dictionary definition of "out of centre," when applied to humans, makes me ask questions. The centre of what? Who sets the centre? Perhaps it is a good thing to be out of. John Stuart Mill certainly thought so.

"Eccentricity has always abounded," he wrote, "when and where strength of character has abounded; and the amount of eccentricity in a society has generally been proportional to the amount of genius, mental vigour, and moral courage which it contained." So I do hope I can be considered an eccentric, though no one has mentioned it yet—to me.

I look up at the sky and know beginnings. I look up at the sky and know music. A bald eagle diving down the wind scale. A gull rising in a cadenza of light. Pine siskins in a lodgepole pine like notes on a score. From the background of cliff and forest come the unfettered songs of robin and wren, warbler and sparrow. Everywhere on the cliff rocks are scattered, with no uniformity at all. Everywhere in the forest there is a wildness of flowers. Trees are accountable only to death. I look all about me and know freedom. . . .

You who read me in newspapers and magazines will have guessed that when I opt for silence and solitude, when I decry "the base, ignoble throng," it is because I like all people only too well. Like? I love them. So we talk on the patio or in my living-room and little gets written, not enough produce gets picked, few of the typewriter, barn, and house chores get attended to when they should be. This may go on day after day in summer. Add to it my frequent absences on Regional Board business and you have a real problem. Papers and dust pile up, money doesn't come in, and I get to the stage that if one more boat heads this way I'll take to the high hills. Where the only difference would be that guests would arrive by helicopter! . . .

How many more minds shall I refresh if I write it down instead of speaking it? Will there be anything left to say, in any manner, if the soil goes dry from too much uttering? This never seems to happen when I write, but only when I talk. When there have been too many people for too long. I give them the most precious thing I have: my time.

"Time," said Carl Sandburg, "is the coin of your life and only you can determine how it will be spent. It is the only coin you have. Be careful lest you let other people spend it for you."

My coin time is spinning by and the books are not written. Only the words are said: water that may refresh some one person for a moment before it runs away to Lethe. So we sit on my patio and I look around at all the friendly faces and I love them. I wish they would never go. I wish they would go this minute.

Looking back over the past years I think of the friends who tell me that I should have spent them doing something else in some other place. Yet I feel that I have done what seemed to need doing by me and in this place. In this protected place. The place about which this book is written. Perhaps two thousand years ago the men of the petroglyphs knew it. Possibly four hundred years ago the men of the pictographs came. More than sixty years have passed since John Poole of England saw the big channel rock and planned to build on it. Now I am here. Walking their trails, beaching my boat in their canoe bays, reading the books John Poole left behind him.

Here life is always pounding at my door or beating in my heart and at no time have I felt it more than this last year. It is a singing and a light, a smile on the lips and stars in the eyes. It is the joy that rises like a flame when I wake up each morning to a new day. It is the peace which lies quietly beside me when the sun goes down. It is all these things and more and even in a world which shakes and jangles with the power thrust of nations and the crying of the homeless, I can still say: "I believe." I believe in good, in happiness, in wisdom and above all in love. I wouldn't have missed these years for a million diamonds.[5]

The bread and butter of "Nature Rambles" continued, but Douglas also published two more collections of poetry in her eighth decade: *Prodigal* (1982), perhaps her finest nature poetry, and *Kodachromes at Midday* (1985). More and more she turned to memory and recollection as the source of her creative power. Although her physical life was restricted, her memory and imagination remained boundless. Reminiscence fuelled her writing and she maintained her voluminous correspondence along with the yearly Christmas Letter.

The other great imperative of Douglas's last years was the protection of her land. As the eighties drew to a close, she was preoccupied with the fate of her property. Rising costs, especially property taxes on 137 acres of waterfront property, along with a diminishing income, made her financial situation ever more precarious. (In 1990 she owed over two thousand dollars for her property tax, while her net income was less than six thousand.) Nevertheless, she refused the old age pension, stating that she would not take it as long as she could provide for herself, and that there were others who needed the money more than she did. She sold most of the few remaining pieces of silver and china from her inheritance, reluctantly took out a mortgage with a close friend, and borrowed from others. All of her assets were tied into her property and all of her love and concern was equally centred on her home. To leave it or lose it at this time of her life was unbearable.

Unable to arrange for the property to become a park or to be taken over by a conservancy organization, she hoped to sell to an individual who would give her tenancy for life and accept stringent covenants forbidding subdivision, roads, and logging on the property. "It is the best I can do for this land I love so much, this dear place that is my home," she wrote in her Christmas letter of 1988. "It is hard to write about it without tears when I think of the deep shoreline which I have loved so long; those current eddies, truculent and strong; this big, grey rock which is a world to me."[6] And a year later: "I realize that the restrictions I have put on building make it difficult to sell, yet I would like to feel that here is one natural whole standing against the tide of development. Wish me luck—before my purse is empty!"[7]

By 1991, Gilean was able to assure friends that she had been able to settle the fate of her beloved Channel Rock. She called this letter "The Year of My Friends," and in it she addressed them for the last time.

Dear Friend—

This letter is written to many people, yet it is also written only to you. While I am writing it my thoughts go to each one of you in turn and you are with me again: talking, laughing or simply silent in understanding. I have never appreciated you so much, understood you so well, loved you so dearly. Hard and bleak as this year has been for me sometimes yet I realize that it has been one of the best years of my life.

So what have I done in this year? My column in the *Victoria Times Colonist* flourishes, though sometimes I feel that it goes up and down like a yo-yo in its moods and fancies. Little by little and bit by bit the historical and autobiographical books are growing—and I with them. The paperwork of living has been handled, though sometimes it is almost overwhelming. The letters—too few!—which could be crammed into limited times have gone out and many guests have come in.

There are times, I admit, when my life seems to be organized to the Nth degree and I want to run out into the forest and leave all the debris of living behind me forever. You know how it is, I am sure. There must have been many times when you felt the same way.

That is what is so delightful about writing these letters: my feeling that everything I say is understood and echoed by someone who has touched my life in one way or another. Who can say after even the zaniest of my declarations: "I understand. Can I help you?"

The land is not sold yet, but Merry Christmas just the same, for I am sure that by the New Year all will be settled and settled well. Yet it is hard to say to this dear place: "I am selling you to save you." But that is true. The contract signed will do all it can to prevent the sacrilege of unlimited logging, of roads romping through, of houses accumulating. That is why there has been this long, frustrating wait—oh, I do hope the sailing will be simple from now on!

It has been rough in spots this year: one problem after another and several didn't wait their turn. You know how it is. I am sure you have had such episodes in your life too. But we shall pull through—and learn by the experience.

I have said too much about myself in this letter and too little about you. I am hoping you will fill in the gaps when you write and that this year I can answer you. Last year I tried—I really did. But, believe me, it has been a good learning year and I am happy to have gone to school again.

My love and good wishes go out to you. Never stop learning, never stop trying. May this be a shining year for all of you and for those you love. My thoughts will be hopping right along beside you.[8]

Despite worries about health and finances, Gilean Douglas was still writing and still celebrating life. In one of her last essays, her weakened condition notwithstanding, Douglas's voice was strong in praise of the delights of the physical world.

ONE THING IS SURE: THE HEAT OF THIS JULY

My two small pools are blue with dawn. The scent of water is hard to believe, so delicately it comes upon the first small breeze of morning. The first breeze of a summer morning: fresh, remote as cloud-cool sky, welcome as joy.

Waves talked of this last night in drowsy undertones, hushing each other when white laughter broke upon the water's fringe of forest bones, because of loon calls and the rusty cra-a-cks of dusk-winged herons waking to declare their watchfulness of all things everywhere.

Now dovelight of ripples burnishes the sea as mice of rain scamper the granite shore. Remote upon dun rocks two ravens pour their patience into profit. Sombrely the clouds spill dawn-grey ashes and, once more, the dove of daylight struggles to be free.

Narcissus and blue hyacinth have gone, their fragrance drifting on the air of spring. Tulips still shed a golden light to clear the springtime mists from my remembering. Once more the rose is queen and my garden blooms with beauty.

My neighbours are responsible for that. They came, more than twenty of them, and a smaller group the next day, to plant and generally coddle my vegetable and flower beds. "Thank you" takes on a new meaning when you have neighbours like that.

So now we are all celebrating this hilarious time. If she were here the dear Nanny of my childhood would shake her wise head and say: "There's many a slip twixt cup and lip, Miss Gilean." She would be right and I have the same feeling. I'll put out my hand to take the lovely lucre and some way, somehow, it won't be there. You'll see. But right now I can dream and scheme and celebrate in imagination—and I certainly will.

There are some weird people in this world. Including me. (I am told that my Scots ancestors said this frequently in their own dialect but the ones I canna bide are those chameleons who keep changing their coat to keep up with the apparel around them. I'm too much the other way; possibly because I don't mind a good argument. If you come in this direction and see a sign— "arguments on request"—you'll know that's where I live.)

Actually I'm writing all this fluffle because I may—just *may*—be able to stop counting pennies in a few months. No, it will be years before I can do that, but in a few months I can, at least, not have to be so meticulous with my arithmetic. I never did like arithmetic and nothing in my recent past has changed that feeling. I'll still have to count the nickels, but at least it will be a change of small change and—who knows?—perhaps one day I'll do it with dimes.

If I seem somewhat frivolous it's because the garden does look so beautiful after the working over it received recently from island friends. Tomorrow more are coming to add some final touches. This wonderful weather we're having is showing off everything in the very best way and I positively purr when I view the result.

But—and there always seems to be a big BUT somewhere—there is never enough time left over for all the writing I want to do and should. I have said that before and it seems more like an excuse each time, but it isn't. I cram every spare moment full of doughty deeds—on paper—and just wish there were more of them.

No, the land is not sold, the money I borrowed from helpful friends cannot be repaid as yet, and when it is I won't be able to believe that the struggle is all over. I'll probably go around trying to pay off everyone I see and wondering why my very best friends keep waving me away. Could it be they know me so well, they now mutter habitually: "Better keep it awhile. You'll need it." I hope not. I really do.

Meanwhile each day blossoms into rose and blue sky. The sea is a backdrop of sapphires and diamonds. Everything seems perfect—except for that niggling feeling that something dark and dislikeable is coming my way. That's what I get for having a Highland grandmother who—they used to tell me—could read the future. I was also told that if I put this feeling down on paper the ill wind wouldn't blow in my direction. Maybe so. Maybe so.

But no matter what is happening or is going to happen I still love this beautiful world and still hope with all my heart that it will pull itself up by its boot straps—as they used to say—and do away with some of the trouble and strife all around us; perhaps in our own house. Life is really so short. Why should we postmark it with quarrels?

As always, I went out to tell my land it will be mine in heart no matter who owns it. As always it received me graciously, but with a twinkle. Now what does this mean? Time will tell and I judge that what it says will amuse me.

Today was such a happy day: one of the few when the telephone doesn't ring, nobody comes, and I can concentrate on my writing without interruption. That gives me such a good feeling of relief and restfulness. But it doesn't happen often.

Today was such a perfect day: not too hot, not too chilly, bright sunshine with incense of summer drifting across the land. Everything is growing like mad. The patio grass was cut only eleven days ago and here it is now almost a foot high. I can hardly believe it, but then there are a lot of things I find it difficult to credit when spring and summer are playing their duet.

Reading of riots I think for the umpteenth time how lucky we are to be here, on this island. We have our disagreements—what would life be without their spice?—but out of them comes some really clever planning, some astute ideas. Our meetings may be hilarious, but they are seldom dull. Maybe once in a blue moon. There is one person I would walk miles to hear when she takes off into the wild blue yonder.

Has anyone been looking at the dawns these days? They are so beautiful. Perhaps a star. Perhaps not. It doesn't seem to matter. There is the great stretch of sky, that D Minor stretch of sea and all around that powerful sense of being part of it all and yet alone. How much I value these moments, hours and, if I'm lucky, even days of separation from everything except the core of life, the soul of being. It is such a vital feeling—I am living, I am living, I am alive at last. What could there be more wonderful than that?

But what can I do with all this vitality? What can I see? Where can I go? As always, I go into the forest. As soon as I step inside its shade and sniff its perfume I relax. All my foreign feelings drop away like a discard of yesterday. I am at home again and as comfortable as a pussy curled up in a big, soft chair. In my big, soft chair, now that I think of it, while I myself perch on a footstool. It just shows you who is the important person around here.[9]

In 1992, Douglas finalized the agreement for the sale of the property under her stipulations. Protecting the property had always been her primary concern, but now having the money to pay her outstanding debts eased her mind greatly and freed her energies for her work. She continued writing her column in 1992, and her final book of poetry, *Seascape with Figures*, appeared that same year. It was in part a reprint of the original volume pubished in 1967, combined with poems from *Prodigal* and new poems. She was also working on two new collections: a sequel to *The Protected Place* and a collection of the coast articles she had written in the fifties. (A third, a collection of character sketches from her time in the mountains, was complete but unpublished.) As she heard time's winged chariot drawing near, she struggled to complete her last two books.

In the fall of 1992, one of her valedictory "Nature Rambles" summed up her love for nature and writing in a column entitled "All I Ever Wanted to Do Was Write." As she drew closer to death, she reaffirmed her lifelong need for and belief in the power of these two forces, which had shaped her destiny and defined her identity.

I could go up this river, just round that white-birched bend and never be seen again; except by the costive sky or the otter kit or the heron with days to spend fishing for rainbows in a heaven the world passed by. I could go into this wood—just past that windfall there—and never be seen again except by the still-faced night or the silken mole or the owl soft-winging where time and the timeless blend into calm, earth-deep delight.

No other world but the moon on a silent, wind-turned tide and sun on sitting stone and rain on a roofing tree; just up this river my labouring heart could hide and in this knowing wood I might den with tranquility.

How good it is to stand under the stars, knowing no more of the world than that it is a round ball rolling in space. Knowing no more of life than that there is death at both ends of it. How simple the world is when taken in small pieces! We can be happy in little chunks and never, perhaps, realize that we have ever been any other way.

"What have you found to be the hardest thing in writing?" asked a friend. Without one second's hesitation I said: "Getting time to write."

Writing is all I have ever wanted to do. It is all I have dreamed of, thought about, cared for. It embraces everything: solitude, silence, the satisfaction of constructing something which I can always be improving. Sometimes I think that it is like going into the opposite form of this human world where there seems to be so little of anything but noise and laughter—which is, too often, not laughter at all but a cry for help.

Talking to a physician the other day—not my physician—he said to me: "Sounds like simple depression." Perhaps it is. We are too inclined to give long names to short stories. Perhaps the drear, dark nights and cloudy days are taking their revenge for the horrid things I have said about them. But perhaps not—and don't let yourself be carried off by that romantic notion. Whatever it is, it's a nuisance and should be done away with. It does seem to me that we have more than enough nuisances in this world.

I must admit that, whatever the reason for them, I am fed up to the teeth with these damp, dark days. Who wants to fall over their own feet while trying to get out of the house? Who wants to lunge against a hard, ungiving door when you expected an airy space? This is, without a doubt, the most contrary winter I have encountered in a long time and I could do much better with its space than its company.

I must say that I feel considerably heartened after making those nasty remarks. All is not lost. The grass will green, the flowers will blue, and somehow or other we'll get through. But for all our sakes, sun, hurry it along. I have practically forgotten what you look like. Imagine the consternation if someone pointed you out and I said: "What's that?" Besides, what heavenly good is it going to do me at night? You have to think of all those things, you know.

I look towards the west and there is only a black cloud of mill smoke covering the white snow of the mountains. It fringes north and south. In the east I stand upon the big rock which forms the foundation of my home and garden. I look out to sea and to the islands beyond and wish for the impossible: that this lovely land might be again as I first knew it.

Inside the telephone rattles with people and the room looks as though not one hurricane, but half a dozen had recently paid a visit. I am trying to get at least one short piece of writing completed, but even that small effort is frustrated. Was every Christmas and New Year like this? Surely not. I couldn't have survived it. Whatever the malaise is that haunts the world these days it is a stranger to me and I don't like any part of it.

Here it is only March and already I am lamenting the new year. What am I thinking about? Soon it will be my birthday and trees will be budding and birds positively bursting with the songs they can't sing yet. Surely, surely then the sun will come again and everything be full of wonder and exhilaration. But there will be quietness too. Perhaps when the moon comes sailing gently over the house and the air is so still that you could almost hear a wish forming. A wish for peace.

I look out into the darkness which is so soft and seeable. It is like deep velvet on the roughness of the world. You can hide in it, confide to it, tell it your troubles. This time when winter has gone, but spring is hardly here, seems so calm and beautiful that I could wish it might last forever.[10]

Through the winter and spring of 1992–1993, Douglas's health degenerated. Edwards provided the constant care she now needed. In the spring, she was airlifted to the Campbell River Hospital, where she stayed for several weeks. Despite her dreadfully weakened condition, she continued to exert her charm. The pilot, young enough to be her grandson, was so enchanted by her that he took the time to visit her during her stay in hospital.

Finally, she was strong enough to journey back to Cortes. She now had money to hire a team of round-the-clock caregivers, and she wanted to die at home, on her beloved island. Although she was no longer able to write during her last summer, Douglas often talked of the book she was working on. Her body was, as she put it, composting around her, yet she was determined not to die until her work was done.

Two days before her death, she told a friend that the book was finally complete. Her body felt quite different that day, she said—not a feeling she could explain but something she had never felt before. But, she said, she was happy. It seemed she had finished the internal narrative of her life.

On October 31, surrounded by friends, Gilean Douglas's life closed. She slipped peacefully out of her body at the dusk of that golden autumn day with a full moon rising. It was a fitting hour of death. October 31 was a day of spirit and imagination she had always revered, and the month of October was always a time of recollection and reflection for Douglas, "the month we count our blessings, before the light dies and all the songs depart."[11] She often wrote of autumn's beauty shadowed by death, and some of her words seem to foreshadow her own death. "A 'prelude to death' has been said to describe October. In that case how wonderful is dying! Embers of Indian summer glowing, Venus all glorious in the twilight sky . . . then the brave scarlet of the Hunter's moon, rising at sundown and staying all night with us . . . The Hunter's moon follows the same path as the springtime sun, and here again is the eternal circle of life and death."[12]

THE HARD THING

This will be the hard thing—
leaving tree and sky,
leaving hill and garden
when I die.

Not the failing vision,
not the shattered breath,
but—will there be a spring wind
after death?[13]

The journey over, Gilean Douglas's body was wrapped in a handwoven shawl and placed in a coffin filled with autumn leaves. After her remains were cremated, the ashes were returned to her beloved Channel Rock for eventual burial. A memorial service was held for island friends in the community hall to mark her passing. In spring, another ceremony, attended by many from off the island as well as local residents, marked the interment of her ashes in a place on her property many thought had been named by Douglas in her poem "I Have Lived with These":

and my small dust will find the tender rain
and lie in rest below the singing trees.

Epilogue

THE FAIRING

The faint, delicate streaks and strays of sunlight spotted through the December forest are like the fading footsteps of the year. Empty nests, blank sky, grey plants, dark trees—but a winter wren is singing. A pileated woodpecker, drilling into a tree for hibernating insects, taps out an accompaniment. Each sound, each sight, of these last days fills me with happiness.

This is my fairing. When my grandmother was young each Fair meant a fairing: a gift from the Fair for someone you loved. The custom was no longer followed when I first heard about it, but I followed it. Somehow it seemed only right that I, who was receiving so generously, should give my little too.

So here is my fairing for you. A gift from the great Fair of life. A small song of our dark and bright years.

You were old when I first met you. The defiles of laughter, the canyons of buried tears, had petroglyphed your face to ancient beauty. I looked at you and I loved you, right from that first moment. I shall love you until I die.

When I was barely able to walk I remember staggering across the lawn, my arms wide open as I tried to take all of you into them at once. I fell against you, I breathed your perfume, I knew even then that when I had you, I had everything.

I was an only child and I might have been lonely—but how could I be lonely when you were always with me? We played together under the big elm and up the silver maple. For all your age you were lithe as the wind, bright as a sun-topped morning. When I fell from fences and trees you caught me and hushed my crying. With you I warmed my childhood at the fire of autumn and jumped with joy of the stars.

There was no communication gap between us—never, never! I told you everything and you understood before I had spoken. I was orphaned when very young, but the look and touch of you could make me forget that I was all alone in the world. Because of you I could smile and hold my head high. Because of you courage ran through my veins and only you saw my tears.

Then I grew older and we grew apart. No, not that, not really. But work and new friends and new loves filled my thoughts. City streets mesmerized with their magic of movement. City lights glittered promises. I lost weight and grew pale and was restless as traffic. Everywhere ended in nowhere. All things were zeros.

Why? Why? But I knew. You said nothing and the unspoken filled me. You sang a song of my teens and I trembled. You played a nursery tune and my smogged days tumbled down. I ran over them crying for you. You were more than new friends and new lovers; more than money or power or hand-clapping. You were truth and first love and fulfillment. Endless, for ever and always.

Our reunion. How well I remember that high-lying, mount-crowned valley filled with the tansy of summer. The winter-deep snows sparked with moonlight. The dawns and the days and the sunsets, each one filled with wild friendship and beauty. Each one Christmas, Birthday, Thanksgiving.

Then the flaming sword of fire, driving me out of Eden. Back to the smoke and the asphalt. So many days wasted in worry. So many months lost to pretending. You know it, you know it! The frustration, grief, but never quite despair. The desperate urge that brought its own release. The friends that were not, the love that never was.

You know it has never been easy. Not since the long days of childhood. Death was always a neighbour and misunderstanding lived just down the street. But when sorrow, want, illness, or cruelty came I dived into the thought of you as into the Pool of Siloam. I drew your coolness around me. You brought me out of the desert into the promised land; let me grow into joy of it. More joy than speech or writing could ever tell.

You have been called by many names: nature, spirit, subconscious, creation, wilderness, and more. No one name can contain you. You are all and yet none of them. Perhaps you are God, Manitou, Saghalie Tyee. To me you are under, over, all around. You are in everything I see, hear, touch, smell, taste. Especially you are in the beauty of wind, water and light. In silence, solitude and that sure knowing of wilderness and wild things. It is our not knowing of our vital need for you that may destroy us in the end.

This is December and Christmas is in it. Every day is Christmas for me, but today let me give you a gift of my greetings. Because of the big loon that is calling now from Nika Bay and the heron on Mahtlinnie Rock. Because of the juncos skimming down to the feeding place and the black brant going up in a lilt of white foam. Because of the wolves, two whelps and their mother, that I can hear and see on Marina Island, playing together on the beach sands in all the wild innocence of morning.

Thank you for giving me these gifts beyond measure and the good sense to value them. For bringing me friends who prize them too. Let my words written here, this fairing, be my inadequate gift to you who was with me when I was born and will be with me when I die. Who has brought light into darkness and turned water into wine.[1]

Gilean Douglas, 1984.

PHOTO: GEORGE SIRK

Notes

CHAPTER 1

[1] Unless otherwise noted, all quotations in Chapter 1 are from *A February Face.*

Gilean Douglas began writing this manuscript, her unpublished auto-biography, in the 1940s but never finished it; it ends in her mid-twenties. The manuscript is stored along with all of Gilean Douglas's other papers and all of her photographs at the University of British Columbia Library in the Special Collections and Archives Division. Unless otherwise apparent, all photographs were taken by Douglas. Captions in quotation marks are Douglas's words.

For the convenience of those who may wish to refer to the original sources at the UBC Library, references to Gilean Douglas texts are coded where appropriate by box and file numbers; *A February Face* is 6-11 (Box 6, File 11).

[2] Throughout this book we refer to Gilean Douglas in various ways, depending upon the context. As is standard procedure, we use only her surname, Douglas, whenever we talk about her as a public person, as a writer, or when she herself is reflecting upon her past life or work. When we discuss her in personal relationships we use her first name, Gilean, and we also use the first name of the other person(s) in the relationship. We use her full name at the start of chapters or after significant changes in a chapter.

[3] Newspaper clippings (Gilean Douglas fonds, scrapbook).

[4] "Once Upon a Christmas" (Gilean Douglas fonds 6-5). Published as "Best Wishes 'Flying Your Way,'" *Victoria Times Colonist* "Nature Rambles" column, 22 December 1991.

Note: Throughout this book, all extracts from Douglas's articles are derived from her manuscript versions, located in the fonds as indicated.

[5] "The Little Colonel's Good Times Book" (Diary) (Gilean Douglas fonds).

[6] Letter from the "Battle Maid" to her newspaper club, *Toronto News*, date unknown (Gilean Douglas fonds, scrapbook).

[7] "The Little Colonel's Good Times Book."

[8] Diary entry, 1920 (summarizing the previous year) (Gilean Douglas fonds).

[9] "Exit," in *Poetic Plush.*

CHAPTER 2

1. *A February Face* (Gilean Douglas fonds 6-11).
2. Letter from Gilean Douglas to *Calgary Herald*, 5 February 1946 (Gilean Douglas fonds 24-4).
3. *A February Face.*
4. "Gypsy Weather," in *Kodachromes at Midday.*
5. "The Romance of New Mexico" (Gilean Douglas fonds 34-12). Published under the same title in *Motor Camper & Tourist*, February 1926.
6. "Goitre Changed My Life" (Gilean Douglas fonds 3-25). Published under the same title in *Canadian Home Journal*, September 1952.
7. "Goitre Changed My Life."

CHAPTER 3

1. Letter from Roy Wilson, 9 March 1928 (Gilean Douglas fonds 23-16).
2. Letter from Betty Rittenhouse, 24 January 1928 (Gilean Douglas fonds 18-25).
3. "Sierra Song," in *Prodigal.*
4. "Goitre Changed My Life" (Gilean Douglas fonds 3-25). Published under the same title in *Canadian Home Journal*, September 1952.
5. Post-nuptial agreement with Eric Altherr (Gilean Douglas fonds 33-13).
6. "Goitre Changed My Life."
7. Letter from Louise Meginness, 4 June 1934 (Gilean Douglas fonds 18-1).
8. "When April," in *Kodachromes at Midday.*
9. "Can You Marry and Live?" (Gilean Douglas fonds 4-14). Written and sent out in 1948 under pseudonym Grant Madison, but apparently never published.

CHAPTER 4

1. "Song against Hate," in *Now in This Night.*
2. "When I Look Back," in *Now in This Night.*
3. Diary entry, 6 January 1942 (Gilean Douglas fonds).
4. "Wilderness Love Story," in *River for My Sidewalk.*
5. *A February Face* (Gilean Douglas fonds 6-11).
6. Excerpt from "Nature Poets in Now," in *Prodigal* (reprinted in *Seascape with Figures*).
7. "The Woman Speaks" (Gilean Douglas fonds 2-5). Published under the same title in *The Meriden Record*, 2 March 1939.
8. The following is Gilean Douglas's list of sources for quotations used in "Home," a chapter from *Silence Is My Homeland*:

   "Let the fields and gliding streams . . ."—Virgil, *Georgics.*
   "It is a comfortable feeling . . ."—Anthony Trollope, *The Last Chronicles of Barset.*
   "However small it is on the surface . . ."—Charles Dudley Warner, *My Summer in a Garden.*

"There is no season . . ."—William Browne, "Variety."
"Every man hath in his own life . . ."—Jeremy Taylor, *Holy Living.*
"Never any more to hurry . . ."—David Grayson, *Adventures in Solitude.*
". . . after we have made the just reckoning . . ."—William Rena, "Some Fruits of Solitude."
"The soul selects her own society . . ."—Emily Dickinson, "Exclusion."
"Henceforth I ask not good fortune . . ."—Walt Whitman, *Leaves of Grass.*

CHAPTER 5

1 "Life," in *Now in This Night.*
2 "Wilderness Love Story," in *River for My Sidewalk.*
3 "February Footnotes," in *River for My Sidewalk.*
4 "Bush Map," in *Prodigal* (reprinted in *Seascape with Figures*).
5 "Guest Rules" (Gilean Douglas fonds 30-16).
6 "Merry Christmas to All," in *River for My Sidewalk.*

CHAPTER 6

1 The following are Gilean Douglas's sources given for quotations used in "Sun in the Valley," a chapter from *Silence Is My Homeland*:

   ". . . there is no ancient gentlemen but gardeners"—Shakespeare, *Hamlet.*
   "Doubtless God could have made a better berry . . ."—Isaak Walton, *The Compleat Angler.*

2 "Wilderness Winter," in *Silence Is My Homeland.*
3 Letter to Fran Dietrich, 6 May 1947 (Gilean Douglas fonds 24-5).
4 Letter to Louise Meginness, 6 May 1947 (Gilean Douglas fonds 24-11).
5 "Lost Eden" (Gilean Douglas fonds 3-3). Published under the same title in *Nature Magazine*, April 1953.

CHAPTER 7

1 "Old Prospector," written on Keats Island, May 1947, later published in *Seascape with Figures.*
2 Letter to Philip Major, 16 April 1948 (Gilean Douglas fonds 22-1).
3 "We Are the Lucky Ones," in *The Protected Place.*
4 Letter to Philip Major, 25 February 1948 (Gilean Douglas fonds 22-1).
5 Undated letter to Philip Major (Gilean Douglas fonds 22-1).
6 "The Where and What of Whaletown" (Gilean Douglas fonds 2-15). Apparently unpublished essay.
7 "Life without Gadgets" (Gilean Douglas fonds 13-12). Revised version of article originally published as "Canadian Widow Enjoys Her Life" by Jill McClean, *Seattle Times*, 21 June 1964.
8 Diary entry, 24 October 1949 (Gilean Douglas fonds).
9 *Ibid.*

10 Diary entry, 21 October 1949 (Gilean Douglas fonds).
11 "Exile End," in *Seascape with Figures.*
12 Diary entry, 19 November 1949 (Gilean Douglas fonds).
13 Diary entry, 11 November 1949 (Gilean Douglas fonds).
14 "Refugee," in *Now in This Night.*
15 Undated letter to Philip Major (Gilean Douglas fonds 22-1).
16 "Warning," in *Kodachromes at Midday.*
17 "Slow Weather," in *Seascape with Figures.*

CHAPTER 8

1 "Winter Day" (Gilean Douglas fonds 13-12). Revised version of article originally published as "January Storm at Channel Rock," *Victoria Daily Colonist* "Nature Rambles" column, 30 January 1966.

2 "Dock For Their Doorstep" (Gilean Douglas fonds 11-1). Revised version of article originally published as "Home on the Waves," *Family Herald* (Montreal), 5 October 1961.

3 "Seeding by the Saltchuck" (Gilean Douglas fonds 11-1). Revised version of article originally published as "Salt Chuck Gardeners," *Vancouver Sun*, 6 June 1952.

4 "Best Port in a Storm" (Gilean Douglas fonds 11-1). Revised version of article originally published as "Bull Harbour—Fine Port in a Storm," *Sea and Pacific Motor Boat*, December 1952.

5 "The World Belongs to Cool Enthusiasts" (Gilean Douglas fonds 5-13). Published as "Column Fodder on Brink of Changing Hands," *Victoria Times Colonist* "Nature Rambles" column, 7 June 1992.

6 Christmas letter, 1961 (Gilean Douglas fonds 6-8).

7 "Three Come Home," in *The Protected Place.* The entire chapter is reproduced; ellipses are in the original.

8 Letter to Mrs. D. W. Thompson, Canadian Writers' Foundation, 6 November 1962 (Gilean Douglas fonds 28-4).

9 Letter from Canadian Writers' Foundation, 13 December 1963 (Gilean Douglas fonds 28-4).

10 "The Poet Defies," *Now in This Night.*

11 Christmas letter, 1969 (Gilean Douglas fonds 6-8).

CHAPTER 9

1 Christmas letter, 1971 (Gilean Douglas fonds 6-9).

2 Director's Report, Regional District of Comox-Strathcona—Electoral Area I, April 1975 (Gilean Douglas fonds 8-1).

3 "Good Lord Deliver Us," in *The Protected Place.*

4 Director's Report, Summer 1977 (Gilean Douglas fonds 8-1).

5 Director's Report, Year-end, 1975 (Gilean Douglas fonds 8-1).

6 Christmas letter, 1970 (Gilean Douglas fonds 6-9).

7 Christmas letter, 1971 (Gilean Douglas fonds 6-9).

8 "Portrait of June," in *The Protected Place.*

9 "She Killed Grant Madison," *Vancouver Sun*, 15 September 1983.

10 "The Very Sap of Summer," in *The Protected Place.*

11 "My Black Frosty," in *The Protected Place.*

CHAPTER 10

1 Christmas letter, 1968 (Gilean Douglas fonds 6-8).

2 "The Years Have Surprised Me" (Gilean Douglas fonds 5-2). Published under the same title in *Victoria Daily Colonist* "Nature Rambles" column, 6 January 1980.

3 Christmas letter, 1984 (Gilean Douglas fonds 6-10).

4 "I Have Lived with These," in *Seascape with Figures.*

5 "Who Am I?" (Gilean Douglas fonds 13-11). Revised version of article possibly originally published as a "Nature Rambles" column.

6 Christmas letter, 1988 (Gilean Douglas fonds 6-10).

7 Christmas letter, 1989 (Gilean Douglas fonds 6-10).

8 Christmas letter, 1991 (Gilean Douglas fonds 6-10).

9 "One Thing Is Sure: The Heat of This July" (Gilean Douglas fonds 5-15). Published as "Every Little Breeze Seems to Whisper at Ease," *Victoria Times Colonist* "Nature Rambles" column, 8 July 1992.

10 "All I Ever Wanted to Do Was Write" (Gilean Douglas fonds 5-6). Published under the same title in *Victoria Times Colonist* "Nature Rambles" column, 1 March 1992.

11 "October Leaves No Time for Regrets" (Gilean Douglas fonds 5-23). Published under the same title in *Victoria Times Colonist* "Nature Rambles" column, 1 October 1989.

12 "Angel of the North Star" (Gilean Douglas fonds 5-23). Published under the same title in *Victoria Times Colonist* "Nature Rambles" column, 4 October 1981.

13 "The Hard Thing," *Seascape with Figures.*

EPILOGUE

1 "The Fairing," final chapter of *The Protected Place.*

Chronology

Published Works

1952   *Now the Green Word* (Poetry). Mill Valley, CA: Wings Press.

1953   *Poetic Plush* (Poetry). Dallas: The Story Book Press.

1953   *River for My Sidewalk* (Nature writing). Published under the pseudonym Grant Madison. Toronto: J. M. Dent & Sons.

1958   *The Pattern Set* (Poetry). Montreal: Quality Press.

1959   *Modern Pioneers* (History of Women's Institutes). Edited by Gilean Douglas. Vancouver, BC: Evergreen Press.

1967   *Seascape with Figures* (Poetry). Iowa City: Prairie Press.

1973   *Now in This Night* (Poetry). Detroit: Harlo Press.

1978   *Silence Is My Homeland* (Nature writing). Published in association with the National Writers' Club. Harrisburg, PA: Stackpole Books and Don Mills, ON: Thomas Nelson & Sons.

1979   *The Protected Place* (Nature writing). Sidney, BC: Gray's Publishing.

1982   *Prodigal* (Poetry). Madeira Park, BC: Harbour Publishing.

1984   *River for My Sidewalk* (New edition). Published under the name Gilean Douglas. Victoria, BC: Sono Nis Press.

1985   *Kodachromes at Midday* (Poetry). Victoria, BC: Sono Nis Press.

1992   *Seascape with Figures: Poems Selected and New.* Victoria, BC: Sono Nis Press.

Over the course of her lifetime, Douglas's prose and poetry were published in countless magazines and newspapers in both Canada and the United States. As well, some of her poems were set to music and published by Schirmers. From 1961 to 1992, Douglas wrote a regular column, "Nature Rambles," for the *Victoria Daily Colonist* (which became the *Times Colonist* in September 1980). Other important venues for her work included: *American Nature, Canadian Home Journal, Canadian Mining Journal, Canadian Poetry, Chatelaine, Dalhousie Review, Family Herald, Forest & Outdoors, Nature Magazine, Ottawa Citizen, Outdoor Canada, Reader's Digest, Saturday Evening Post, Saturday Night, Seattle Times, Toronto Star, Vancouver Sun*, and *The Villager*.

Gilean Douglas Poetry

from Sono Nis Press

Limited quantities of these classic works available!

- ❦ *Kodachromes at Midday*
    ISBN 0-919203-70-1 · Paper · 75 pp. · $9.95

- ❦ *Seascape with Figures: Poems Selected and New*
    ISBN 1-55039-015-5 · Paper · 96 pp. · $9.95

A DIVISION OF
MORRISS PUBLISHING LTD.

TELEPHONE (250) 598-7807
FAX (250) 598-7866

P. O. BOX 5550
STATION B
VICTORIA, BRITISH COLUMBIA
CANADA V8R 6S4

sono.nis@islandnet.com
http://www.islandnet.com/~sononis/